"Renee uses a fresh and innovative way to engage the reader while making readers feel like they are meeting their new best friend. She walks readers through the stages of life and focuses her words on the importance of a person's relationship with Jesus Christ. This is a must read for women of all ages!"

—**Jennifer Bignotti**, Artist

I0528210

Praise for *Hey, Mom, God's Not Done with You Yet!*

"This book is a must read for all moms as we navigate through the many seasons of life. Rence does an amazing job of inspiring and connecting to the reader with wit, relatable life stories, and encouraging words of advice and scripture that affirms God is always by our side at every turn through the celebrations and 'deserts' we may experience. Enjoy pausing, reflecting, and connecting with Him, yourself, and those you hold most dear." ♥

—**Cindy Grice**, Ohio Middle School Principal

"Renee takes you on an authentic, heartfelt journey through the various phases of motherhood. The open door into her triumphs and struggles gives you a refreshing and powerful take on being a woman, a mother, and a child of God. You end the book hopeful and energized, ready to take on life with Jesus leading your way."

—**Melissa Gill,** Accountant and Photographer

"Renee Chenevey is one of the most spiritually focused and purposeful moms I know! You will love her insights and humor. Reading this game plan plus personal testimony will be such an encouragement—it's like Renee is holding your hand through the ups and downs of motherhood! I join her in the empty nester phase, but I wish I had this book to read in my earliest parenting years! Renee communicates with authenticity and bold truth. Her stories are relatable (and true, as I walked alongside her in many of these seasons). Reading Renee's book, I was encouraged that I am not alone . . . I also laughed and enjoyed the stories and had much to ponder in between. This book is a must-read for any mom."

—**Stephanie McAllister**, Discipleship & Women's Ministry,
Freshwater Community Church

"A perfect blend of mother, mentor, and minister, Renee weaves a heartfelt, interactive roadmap for Christ-centered parenting that will encourage, educate, and embolden mothers of any age to step out in faith wielding the Word of God as they take on the most difficult and the most important job of all!"

—**Rachel Whitehawk Day**, Founder, Whitehawk Institute
for Cognitive Resilience

"Renee's honest and transparent journey through motherhood is refreshing and encouraging. The 'Dance Pauses' and journaling spaces brought a smile and lightheartedness as the Lord spoke through her words to my heart. Because Hey Mom, God's Not Done with You Yet is structured so beautifully, all women can gather, read, and see themselves in the telling of Renee's story."

—**Karen Galehouse**, Author of *Boo Boo Bunny and Friends,*
The Color of Feelings

"With engaging and passion-filled communication, Renee's authenticity and nontraditional writing style captivates her audience. There is something to be learned for every season of life, and with Renee's unique ability to champion other mothers, readers will feel inspired and empowered. A must read."

—**Angel Porubsky**, Co-Lead Pastor, Radiant Life Church,
Wadsworth, OH

"Renee's words are like a warm hug—relatable and encouraging! She mixes Scripture, humor, and joy to remind you that you're not alone in this journey of motherhood. Her 'God Pauses' are perfectly timed, and the song selections will lift your spirits. If you're looking for a little sanity and a lot of grace, *Hey Mom, God's Not Done with You Yet* is exactly what you need!"

—**Ruth G. Crane**, Executive Director & Founder,
Ears To You, A 501 (c)(3) Nonprofit

Hey, Mom,
GOD'S NOT DONE WITH YOU YET

Navigating You Through the Seasons of Life

RENEE CHENEVEY

*inspire*books

Published by Inspire Books
www.inspire-books.com

Interior Design by Jose Pepito
Cover Illustration by Hayden Chenevey

Paperback ISBN: 978-1-961065-21-5
Hardback ISBN: 978-1-961065-22-2
Ebook ISBN: 978-1-961065-23-9
Library of Congress: 2024924006

Printed in the United States

This book is dedicated to my mom, Dee, who inspired me to write this book! She refocused herself through all the seasons of her life, chose to keep laughing in spite of the painful stuff, and encouraged me in my journey as a mom.

Contents

Foreword

It is both an honor and a privilege to write the foreword for my dear friend Renee's first book, Hey Mom, God's Not Done with You Yet! What a beautiful and timely message this is for every mom (like me) who has ever questioned her worth, impact, or the path she's walking. Renee's words radiate encouragement, reminding us that no matter where we are in life, God is always at work, and His plans for us are far from finished.

I first met Renee years ago through a mutual friend who introduced her to my Bible study. Little did I know, that moment would lead to a deep and lasting friendship. Our paths reconnected through Facebook Messenger, of all places, when I asked her if she would be interested in joining our local prayer hub meeting. Renee said yes to joining us monthly at my home to pray for our nation, community, families, marriages, schools, leaders, and churches (to learn more, visit www.HerVoiceMVMT.com). Since then, my life has been profoundly blessed by her presence. Renee's heart for the Lord, her passion for prayer, and her unwavering faith have inspired me in ways words can scarcely capture.

As a mother of four grown sons who all love and serve the Lord, Renee is a living testimony to God's faithfulness. She has poured her heart and soul into raising her boys, guiding them with wisdom, love, and grace. But beyond her role as a mother, she is an incredible wife to her husband, Jeff, a wonderful mother-in-love to Nadia and Elizabeth, an amazingly fun Grammy to her three grandbabies, and a true friend to so many of us. Renee's example of steadfast faith and love has not only shaped her family but has also touched the lives of everyone blessed to know her, including me.

This book is more than a message for moms; it is a powerful reminder that we are never too young, too old, too tired, or too far gone for God to continue working in us. Renee has walked through life with authenticity, humility, and grace, and now she invites us to join her on a journey of growth and empowerment. Get ready to laugh, pause, dance, praise, and discover more of who God says you are. For some of you, God's just getting started!

As you turn these pages, my prayer is that you, too, will be encouraged to embrace the truth that God is not done with you yet. No matter what season of life you're in, He has more in store for you—more growth, more joy, and more purpose than you can imagine.

Thank you, Renee, for sharing your story, your heart, and your obedience with us. Your words will inspire and uplift, just as your friendship has done for so many of us over the years.

With love and admiration,
Your joy-filled, prayer-warring friend,
Amy S. Dudley
Author of *Walk It Out*

Introduction

I wasn't always a mom. In fact, I wasn't always a wife. I was just me. I know it's hard to believe, but it's true. There was a "me" before all this "stuff," albeit good; it pushed "me" behind the scenes. So, who was me?

Well, maybe that is where I should start, but I don't want this book to be only about me. That could really get boring, and who wants to be bored? I want you to get to know you too. So, why not come on a journey with me as I share the happy and sad of figuring out "me" through this roller coaster called life? Are you ready?

I know it could get scary. It could get revealing. It could be an "in-your-face" kind of discovery, but that's a good thing. What have you got to lose? A better knowledge of who you are and who you can be? Sounds pretty good.

Listen, I don't have all the answers, but I sure can give you some advice from a seasoned mommy veteran—or at least from a mom who has battle wounds from over a quarter century of marriage and kids.

You do matter. You do have an assignment to accomplish in your life—maybe many assignments—in fact, a lifetime of making your mark on this world. Being a mom is an awesome thing, and if done well, it may seem it's all you need to do to have done well.

But what about you? What are your dreams? Have they been buried under stacks of laundry, homework, schedules, and Zoom calls? Well, now's the time to figure out some things.

No matter where you are on your journey, I hope my story helps you know you have worth no matter what "chapter" you are in. You might think you want to be done. But you are still here. You might think it's too late for your dreams. But you are still here. You might think it's impossible to find YOU. But you are still here, and, you know, Mama, that means God's not done with you yet!!

Chapter 1

The Great Adventure Begins

Jesus, undeterred, went right ahead and gave his charge: "God authorized and commanded me to commission you: Go out and train everyone you meet, far and near, in this way of life, marking them by baptism in the threefold: Father, Son, and Holy Spirit. Then instruct them in the practice of all I have commanded you. I'll be with you as you do this, day after day, right up to the end of the age."
—Matthew 28:18–20, MSG

♪ DANCE PAUSE ♫
"The Great Adventure," Steven Curtis Chapman

D o you ever find you have a song in your head, and if you think of it early in the day, it stays there all day, permeating your every move, your every bathroom break, and every hand washing? Yeah, that happens to me a lot. "The Great Adventure" is one of those songs that I often sang in my twenties. I could visualize myself in the Wild West, riding my strong, majestic horse into the dusty tumbleweeds to pan for gold and place my flag marker (Go back and do the DANCE PAUSE above to get the full experience before moving on).

Yes, I could dream big, but you know, this one thing often got in my way—FEAR. Fear of failure. Fear of not being good enough. Ever been there? Well, that ugly tactic of an unmentionable being often tried to cripple me, but I am alive and well to tell you today that the jerk-devil (I said it!!) loses in the end, and the Bible says that "greater is he that is in you, than he that is in the world" (1 John 4:4, KJV). Basically saying, fear is a liar and doesn't have anything on us—if we don't let it. So, that's where I will begin my story.

A long, long time ago, in a galaxy far away . . . no, not that long ago, but I just threw that in for all those Star Wars fans out there. A few decades ago, I started off after college to make my HUGE mark on the world. You know, make it a better place—yada, yada, yada. Then, some realities happened, and it's not as easy as the recent YouTube generation. I had to work hard and stay the course when the course was hard to see or when it had obstacles too big to move on my own.

Obstacles, you say? Why, yes! Those sometimes ridiculously enormous "things" that keep us from taking that next step forward. I made it through four years of school at Grove City College in Pennsylvania, and it was a tough journey, let me tell you! The academics were no joke. I worked hard, but, most of all, I discovered what it really meant to be a daughter of God, to be loved not in my doing but just in my being. Do you get that? It's not the "earn-your-love" kind of thing, but the unconditional love that just is because God created you. Take a moment and let that TRUTH sink in. See you back in sixty seconds!

(God Pause!)

Ah, welcome back! Discover anything? Would you mind jotting it down right here? Yes, right here in this book! I am a strong believer in interacting with your life and learning (definitely the English teacher coming out in me!). Here's some space to think about that TRUTH that **you are good enough** just because God created you . . .

_____

_____

_____

_____

In the beginning, God created . . . He created all kinds of things, but He especially created YOU. Genesis 1:27 says, "So God created man in his own image, in the image of God he created him; male and female he created them." So, you get He created, right? ☺ Further along in the Old Testament is a verse all about how He specifically created you. Psalm 139:13–16 really speaks to this beautifully:

> *For you formed my inward parts; you knitted me together*
> *in my mother's womb. I praise you, for I am fearfully*
> *and wonderfully made. Wonderful are your works; my soul*
> *knows it very well. My frame was not hidden from you,*
> *when I was being made in secret, intricately woven in the*
> *depths of the earth. Your eyes saw my unformed*
> *substance; in your book were written, every one of them,*
> *the days that were formed for me, when as yet there was*
> *none of them.*

Knitted together in your mama's womb! Imagine the grandmas of old who made intricately knitted blankets and see the detail and care taken in that blanket. Just imagine the hands of the God of the universe forming you! Is it time for another pause? I really think so. Jot down some things going through your mind below, and meet me back here in a few minutes. Ready, set, go . . .

_____

_____

_____

_____

Excellent job!! So, as you can see, this isn't your normal "self-help" book, nor is it a regular Bible study. It's going to be a little untraditional, but I think it's time to shake up your "normal" way of doing and learning things and see what happens.

Okay, so let's get back to me—yeah, this book is all about me. Ha ha ha! No, it better not be. It's about what God did through me, and in that, I can now tell you some things to help you on your own journey as a mama. So, after college, I thought getting a job would be soooooo easy.

Think back to 1992—oh, wait, some of you most likely were not even born, but just pretend, or better yet, Google "1992" so you can really set the stage! Ever heard of the song "Achy Breaky Heart"? Billy Ray Cyrus made a killing with this song in 1992, along with The Cure's "Friday I'm in Love." Top Christian songs were 4Him's "The Basics of Life" and Amy Grant's "Breath of Heaven (Mary's Song)."

Feel free to sing along as you read the rest of this chapter now. I know you want to, so go ahead. See if any of those songs ring a bell. I'll continue to describe what it was like to leave college after four years and journey back to a life at home.

I remember all the headlines for finding a teaching job in 1992. Everyone was saying to me, "Just go be a sub. That's the only way you can really land a teaching job now." More than one person said this to me, but I didn't want to believe it. I prayed and prayed, thanking God I wouldn't have to take the subbing route. It was discouraging, but I kept at it. Then, one day, I received a call from Canfield Schools in Canfield, Ohio. It was an awesome day! They wanted to interview me for an English teaching position.

I remember preparing a portfolio with lessons I had made, photos I had taken of bulletin boards, and several reference letters. I was ready—ready to jump over the first obstacle to start my great adventure!

The interview went really well, so I was asked back to teach a demo lesson of my choosing—another obstacle! But I was made for this. I prepared for this for four years, and God had placed a knowing in me that I was created for a purpose. And, at this point in my then-young life, I knew being a teacher was it.

I landed the job, which required me to do a bunch of things—computer lab, teaching eighth-grade language arts, coaching track, and creating the first seventh-grade girls' basketball team. Sound exciting or exhausting? Ha ha—for a twenty-two-year-old, it was a piece of cake. Not. But I did have a lot more energy than I have now (but those who know me now would say that might be scary because I am still pretty energetic in my fifth decade of life).

I have to say looking back, the four years I taught and coached in Canfield were some of the best years of my life. I loved it! I loved the messiness of the chaos because, in it, I learned how to let God be God, and He created order out of it for me. He used me to touch my students not only in the classroom and the basketball court but spiritually through Fellowship of Christian Athletes. Every step I took was ordered by Him, and every experience prepared me for the next assignment that God had for me—marriage!

So, this brings us to the end of Chapter 1. What do you think so far? I hope you choose to keep going because I truly believe God gave me the inspiration and words for this book, and in that, I know no matter where you are on this "mama journey," God has some morsel of truth to teach you. And I know you will pick this book up again and again to learn a little, laugh a lot, and maybe even cry a bit.

At the end of every chapter, I would love to review some truths with you by asking some questions. Feel free to answer them in your mind, but if you jot a note down, it will help you remember what you might need to learn better.

CHAPTER 1 QUESTIONS

What verse in the Bible talks about what image you were mirrored after in your creation? Jot that verse here:

Psalm 139 is an excellent psalm to read all the way through, but what do verses 13 through 16 say about how you were formed? How does knowing this make you feel?

What are some dreams you have right now? What are some dreams you had a long time ago that you may have forgotten about?

After you write this down, go find some photos of this dream you have. Place that picture where you will see it every day. Ask the Lord to show you if this is a dream you need to wait on, move on, or act on.

Chapter 2

No More Lonely Nights

Enter Stage Right—Married Life

I found him whom my soul loves.
—Song of Songs 3:4

♪ DANCE PAUSE ♫
"I Love You Always Forever," Donna Lewis

After teaching three years, I thought, *Well, Mr. Right is sure taking his time.* But, you see, Mr. Right was waiting for me to be Mrs. Right. I had a few things to settle up with God before I could take on another human to be my partner in this life. Anything you need to settle with God? Remember Chapter 1 and being made in the image of God? Well, I understood this in theory, but I didn't really think I was that special, nor did I get the whole "identity in Christ" thing.

Let's take a look at this "identity in Christ" foundation a little closer. Psalm 139 reminds us how we were made intricately in our "mother's womb." God made us each with a specific purpose and plan. Sometimes, the messiness of this world can create a fog of this truth and reality, so our job is to dig into God's love letter to us. Yes, the Bible is His love letter to you and to me! It's His inspired words to us, as 2 Timothy 3:16 says, and it helps teach, correct, prepare, and guide us in this life to do what God wants us to do. Even the seasoned veterans reading this—keep digging in! There is always something to learn in EVERY season.

So, the Word is our guide in our identity building. As you search for this understanding of who and whose you are, hang onto this verse: "Now if we are children, then we are heirs—heirs of God and co-heirs with Christ, if indeed we share in his sufferings in order that we may also share in his glory" (Romans 8:17, NIV). We are God's heirs! We have inherited all that Christ came to give us, and as a result of his death, He laid ALL sin, sickness, worry, fear, anxiety, and confusion on the cross. But we have to access and tap into the kingdom he gave to us. Knowing who we are in Christ, we also come to learn our authority. He gave us authority over "all the power of the enemy" (Luke 10:19, NIV), so as we know this, we can recognize and stop the enemy from robbing us of our peace and knowing who we are!

(*God Pause:* Grab your journal or write right here!)

Write out 2 Timothy 3:16 in full and in any version you like. I often use the New Living Translation, but the New International Version is popular too.

Now, read that out loud. Yes, out loud—use your outside voice too; it helps you practice your authority, and the enemy hears you better. Okay, go ahead and read that again—aloud. Good! You got it! Our faith grows through hearing the Word of God (Romans 10:17).

I began to do this in my life more and more. I was enjoying just knowing and loving the Lord when—BOOM! God moved. I walked up the lawn of my future husband on one beautiful July day in 1995. I knew who and whose I was, and I was content completely in Him alone. That's the KEY. If you are reading this and in the beginning season of working or going to school and waiting for Mr. Right, don't spend your time looking. Spend your time going to church, attending Bible studies, and spending time alone with Jesus. When you are content in only Him, that's when you know you are ready.

I met Jeffrey Wayne Chenevey in 1995, and exactly a year later, we were married! When you know, you know. I was twenty-six, and he was twenty-eight; we were both working and living our lives in gratitude for finding each other. It was amazingly fun and hard and good all rolled into one.

We spent our first year loving that we didn't have to drive anywhere to meet each other or figure out when was the next time we would see each other. Our lives consisted of going to work, making dinner, praying together, going to church together, and laughing a lot. Saturdays were times of washing the car, cutting the grass, planting flowers in the summer, and in the winter, we snuggled up by the TV to watch a good movie or go to dinner. We also enjoyed our families, but did I mention our first six months were great? But in month seven, our hearts were broken when my dear stepdad, Karel, passed away very suddenly from what we believe to be an aneurysm.

February 17, 1997, Karel Richard Frantz passed from this life to the next. Jeff and I found ourselves newly married and navigating a very tragic and difficult path of loss. We knew God still had us, but it sent us into a roller coaster of emotions and also changed our roles with my mom.

Are you going through a loss right now? Would you mind sharing it here? What happened? How do you feel about it? What are you doing to help heal?

_____

_____

_____

_____

I know, for me, I definitely cry it out. Jeff, on the other hand, doesn't always cry so easily. He is good if we take time to really talk about the loss, even though he doesn't want to, but in this case, I was really struggling, so I talked more. He loved Karel, too, but I spent seventeen years as his daughter, so my loss was a very deep one. Jeff became my steady rock as we made many, many trips to see my mom to help her with all that comes from the death of a loved one. We held firmly to a few verses:

> *Let us hold unswervingly to the hope we profess,*
> *for he who promised is faithful.*
> *(Hebrews 10:23, NIV)*

> *He will wipe away every tear from their eyes,*
> *and there will be no more death or sorrow or crying or pain.*
> *All these things are gone forever.*
> *(Revelation 21:4, NLT)*

Knowing who we were in Christ helped us press into His Word to know He had a plan to carry us through this, as well as help my mom through her intense grief. It was a hard season for us and a hard way to spend our first year together. However, it was also what God used to build a strong foundation of faith for all the joy that was to come!

CHAPTER 2 QUESTIONS

What does it mean to have your identity in Christ? What does this mean to you? (Use this chapter, but take some time to expand by searching the Scriptures for yourself.)

What are the things the Word of God can teach us? What is the verse that answers this, based on Chapter 2?

Think about your life right at this moment. Is there anything you are carrying that feels heavy? Maybe take a few minutes and write about that, and then find a verse that talks about one promise God says in our hurt and what He does for us.

Remembering who and whose you are is the key in this chapter and in your "chapter" where you become a mama. Being grounded in Christ will keep you rooted as you weather the good, the bad, and the amazing of being a parent, and it was the key for me as I began the beautiful journey of mommyhood.

Chapter 3

You're Pregnant!!

For we are God's masterpiece. He has created us anew in Christ
Jesus, so we can do the good things he planned for us long ago.
—*Ephesians 2:10, NLT*

♪ DANCE PAUSE ♫
"Fingerprints of God," Steven Curtis Chapman

O kay, so let's get real here. I was not one of those little girls who dreamed about being a mom. I don't know why exactly, but I think I was a survivor growing up. My mom would be the first to tell you that life was hard for us, but like her, I am a fighter.

I grew up the youngest of three with two older brothers, one who was nice to me most of the time and the other who taught me every sport I know—but he also teased me mercilessly! I am stronger for it, though, because, as Scripture says, "And we know that God causes everything to work together for the good of those who love God and are called according to his purpose for them" (Romans 8:28, NLT). He also says that what the enemy meant for harm, God uses for good (Genesis 50:20). Basically, those things in our lives that seem really tough and hard are the very things God promises to use to refine and define us so we can do even greater things for Him.

Going back to the little-girl me, I struggled a bit. My parents divorced when I was six, and my mom remarried when I was nine. Life was not all cupcakes and rainbows, as some say. My mom worked hard as an elementary teacher, all while juggling being a mom to three kids.

And let me just say to that single mom reading this right now, "You are doing an amazing job! Don't give up. Don't give in because God sees you and promises to meet all your needs. Just keep the faith."

Being a mom is hard enough with a spouse, but doing it through grieving a marriage and working full-time is a whole other level of challenge. So, when I say it was hard on my mama, it was equally hard as she struggled to juggle the many emotions that this entailed. Peace was not always a part of my every day, but in time, that did come—but that's for another chapter.

It seems that right now would be a good time to stop and pause.

(God Pause)

What's been hard for you in your life? Are there things you are holding onto from when you were a child? Are there hurts and bruises you need to confess to someone or write down right now? Let's take a minute to write some real, raw thoughts and feelings. Don't allow those hurts to hold you captive any longer. One of the greatest things you can do is first acknowledge what has been done to you. Let's start there . . .

Grab that tissue and inhale deeply. Now, let it out slowly. I like to say, "Breathe in the Holy Spirit and breathe out the yuck." Okay, one more time. In . . . and out . . .

Did you know God said He treasures every tear in a jar of alabaster? Psalm 56:8 says, "You keep track of all my sorrows. You have collected all my tears in your bottle. You have recorded each one in your book" (NLT). Ah, so beautiful, right? We'll come back to why I, for some reason, remember that jar as being alabaster, but let's get on with this business of healing our hurts. It's important to get ourselves healthy before wanting to bring a little life into the world.

So, can I give you some advice? Yeah, well, you'll get it whether you want it or not. ☺ I searched my heart in my early twenties, and I found I had some hurts to deal with from living in this world. For me, that meant getting help from a Christian counselor who helped me find hope through forgiveness and letting go . . . and then healing. The scripture says in Psalm 139:23–24 (NLT):

> *Search me, O, God, and know my heart; test me and know*
> *my anxious thoughts. Point out anything in me that offends*
> *you, and lead me along the path of everlasting life.*

There's that Psalm again! So many good things packed in Psalm 139! Asking God to search your heart can be a scary thing, but it's exactly what is needed before you step into parenting. I mean, you can do it in your whole fleshy, worldly self, but the results will be less than favorable. Maybe you have done this before, and maybe you need more than a few lines in this book to process. If you do, then just know it is the best and bravest thing you can do. Facing our hurts and those who hurt us is never easy, but the results are incredibly freeing.

Would you mind just taking a few minutes to think about someone you might need to forgive who hurt you? This could be the first step on your journey. Come, let's do it together. *Thank you, Lord, for helping my friend, your daughter, to release her captor to you. This does not mean what was done to her was right; it just means as she forgives, you also have forgiven her (Ephesians 4:32). We agree right now for the healing that comes when we choose to forgive*

15

and let go. Thank you for healing. Thank you for your wisdom and guidance. In Jesus' name. Amen.

_____

_____

_____

_____

_____

How are you doing? I'm so proud of you, whether you are a seasoned veteran mama or whether you are just starting off. In every step of this journey, we all need to be encouraged that we are on the right track and to keep going. It's worth it!!

(God Pause) Take a walk, stretch your legs, and I'll meet you back here in a few minutes!

Welcome back! I'm just curious—did you grab a snack? If so, what's your go-to snack, or at least today's snack? Feel free to share on my Facebook page (https://www.facebook.com/ReneeCheneveyAuthor). I would love to hear from you!! It's the simple things, right? Let's rejoice and enjoy life:

Taste and see that the LORD is good (Psalm 34:8, NIV).

Having a baby is not the same as waiting for a baby, making a baby, or trying to have a baby, right? Should we unpack all those? Maybe not. Let's just get to the point that Jeff, my husband, and I were twenty-eight and twenty-six when we married. So, we thought: Let's not waste our time but, instead, get on with the business of growing our family if that was what God had for us. So, when I was twenty-seven and Jeff was twenty-nine, we started to think of the timing. We wanted two years together alone, so that meant I could potentially get pregnant in the second year because it would take nine months more for the baby to come. Good thinking, right? We were smart like that.

It took six months to actually conceive, longer than either of us thought it would take, but we did conceive, and on Valentine's Day, almost a year to the day my stepdad passed away, we gave my mom a Valentine that said, "Hi, Grandma!" She cried and cried—so did we. It was a nice way to take a holiday and bring some joy back into it for her. Now, mind you, this was 1998—no social media and no smartphones (all were dumb back then). We let people know with a phone call, an old-fashioned, tell-you-to-your-face interaction. It was fun to share our joy with others!

What happened next? I, of course, grabbed the book of choice back then: *What to Expect When You're Expecting* by Heidi Murkoff, Arlene Eisenberg, and Sandee Hathaway, BSN, as well as another recommended book, *Supernatural Childbirth* by Jackie Mize. Being a teacher and learner, I read and read and read, preparing for what was all new for me as my body became bigger and bigger. Can I tell you I gained fifty pounds? I know, stop eating, woman! I couldn't help it. I was hungry. Nachos Bell Grande and Whoppers were so good! Lol! Thank goodness I was still working out, right? These were my cravings, but I did eat salads and vegetables, so stop judging. But little did I know the child I was feeding would grow to be a football player full of life and joy! Oh, how the Lord loves us so. He orchestrates every little detail of our lives. Can you think of a verse that says just that? Write it down right here:

_____

_____

_____

_____

_____

Read that verse out loud. Now, read it a little slower out loud again. Ah, feeding your spirit is a good thing, Mama. Keep doing that in every season!

(The verse that I wrote out was Psalm 37:23–24. It's one I have often given to my boys as they have ventured off to college and lives of their own.)

On October 8, 1998, after twenty-six hours of labor and three hours of pushing, Hunter Scott Chenevey entered our lives. My body was never the same again. Ha ha! No, seriously, it wasn't, but it was worth every stitch and every hemorrhoid. He weighed in at eight pounds, ten and a half ounces. Every doctor visit, he was in the ninetieth percentile for weight, height, and head circumference! Healthy boy!

It was amazing to become a parent, and I know you understand that whether you conceived a child yourself or you welcomed one home through adoption, foster care, or helping your family. God brings children to us in many ways, and no one way is better than the other. When you take on the mama role, you are never the same again—emotionally, physically, spiritually, or socially. The Lord takes you to a new level of living and dying to yourself, right? Some of that was hard, so I liked having a plan.

My sis-in-love, Kristina, recommended a book called *On Becoming Baby Wise* by Gary Ezzo and Dr. Robert Bucknam. This book impacted my parenting tremendously. I cannot say enough good things about it. I didn't know it in 1998, but I can say now that it helped me guide all four of my boys to sleeping through the night by nine weeks old! Sleeping through the night is seven to eight hours of sleep straight! It was glorious when I slept that much again. I will refer to this book more in later chapters, but it was what helped me keep my sanity as my world changed to taking care of a new little person. As we end this chapter, the greatest advice the authors of *On Becoming Baby Wise* suggest can be found in Chapter 1, which mentions "Achieving Balance." Here's what they said:

- *Life doesn't stop once you have a baby.* It may slow down for a bit, but it should not stop entirely. You do not stop being a daughter, a sister, a friend, or a wife. Remember to maintain those relationships after the baby too.

- *Date your spouse.* This has been a favorite for both of us for over twenty-four years now! Get back in the habit of going out alone again. Your baby will be just fine.

- *Continue those loving gestures you enjoyed before the baby came along.* Enjoy activities you did together before baby, and also remember to treasure your spouse! Get the baby a goodie? Be sure to get your spouse something too.

- *Invite some friends over for food and fellowship.* (Inviting others over forces you to plan your child's day around serving others.)

- *At the end of each day, spend fifteen minutes sitting with your spouse discussing the day's events.* We have continued to have couch time for years now—not always consistently, but we can tell when we don't do it! Do this in front of your children as a visual expression of your togetherness. Share your needs and concerns with each other, and also teach your kids (as they get older) that Mommy or Daddy comes first.[1]

---

[1] Robert Bucknam, MD, and Gary Ezzo, *On Becoming Baby Wise: Giving Your Infant the GIFT of Nighttime Sleep* (Oregon: Multnomah, 1995), 26–27.

CHAPTER 3 QUESTIONS

What does Psalm 56:8 say about how God cares for us? Is He really paying attention? Why?

Find a verse that talks about forgiveness. Why should we forgive according to God? What also does forgiveness do for you, in your own words?

What are a few things the book *On Becoming Baby Wise* says to do to keep a balance after the baby comes?

Chapter 4

Diapers, Diapers, Diapers

No, in all these things we are more than conquerors through Him who loved us.
—*Romans 8:37*

♪ DANCE PAUSE ♫
"Eye of the Tiger," Survivor

P-U!! What's that smell? Oh, that's just my life for many, many years. I really can't smell anything. I have become immune to poop and poop smells. Oh, yes, I believe you, too, can achieve this amazing talent if you try hard enough. You just have to have a bunch of babies close in age, and you will also attain this awesome feat of being able to not smell the stench of poop. What I really can do is hold my breath but still breathe through my mouth, all while not touching or pinching my nose. I know—you are so jealous. It's really an amazing talent, and I was so glad I had this talent from 2000 through 2008!

Hunter enjoyed a glorious life as an only child for only nineteen months. Although short-lived, I know it was appreciated that we had another baby so quickly after he exited the womb. Probably not, but it was God's plan to bring Luke Jeffrey on Mother's Day in the year 2000, supposedly when the world was going to end. (Google that—Y2K was a real thing. Some of the veterans reading will totally get that!)

The world, apparently, did not end, nor did Jesus return (the Bible says no one will know that anyway; we just need to be ready). I am glad it didn't because Luke blessed us on that Mother's Day so long ago. He was born on Sunday, May 14, 2000. It's super easy to figure out how old he is too. What a bonus! His delivery and birth were super easy, too, relatively speaking, in comparison to the full day for Hunter. I pushed only five minutes with Luke all while worship music was playing in the background. Yes, I planned it out so well! But seriously, it did make a difference to have a peaceful atmosphere (and I did get an epidural a lot earlier than I did with Hunter—nothing to prove the second time around!).

I was excited to be a mom again, but I also wondered how I would manage with two now. I also wondered about diapers. Yes, diapers . . . two in diapers! Ahhhhhhh! It was a tag team of chaos and diaper changing every day. I sometimes would sit and cry, thinking this was my life. I know—I knew I was blessed, but I sure didn't feel like it. I felt tired and a little sad during the first sleep-deprived weeks after delivery.

(God Pause!)

Any moms out there felt this way, too? Maybe you are feeling it right now, but don't lose heart, Mama—God is doing a work in you, even now, during all the busyness of being a mom. Isaiah 40:11 talks about this "gentle leading" for mamas. Grab your Bible and write the full verse right here.

What a beautiful image of a shepherd leading "those with young." It makes me think of moms with their young babies and how our Good Shepherd comes alongside us in those hard moments and whispers, "I am with you. I will never leave you. This, too, shall pass" (Deuteronomy 31:6). We grow in the hard times a lot more than the easy, happy times, am I right? Keep the Word of God "hidden in your heart" so that when you are feeling discouraged, you can reach deep down inside for the living Word to lift you up. Like Rocky working hard before one of his matches, you, too, will not only SURVIVE but THRIVE when you embrace the trials. What does God say about trials?

_____

_____

_____

_____

_____

My favorite verse is found in James 1:2–8. Trials test our faith and produce a perseverance in us that helps us become "perfect and complete, lacking in nothing." Right after that, it talks about asking for wisdom. God will give us the wisdom we need in all seasons we are in, and when we are in a trial, we are often being refined. First Peter 1:6–7 also talks about the joy ahead after enduring trials. What else does it say about our faith? What happens to it? What is it compared to in these verses? Please take a moment and jot down your answers here.

_____

_____

_____

_____

_____

So, what did I do to survive? I prayed during breastfeeding, I prayed during diaper changes, and I prayed as I tried to nap and sleep throughout the day. Did I mention we had two dogs, too? But, in my defense, we did get them before babies, and the two together weighed a whopping twenty pounds! Cole was a Lhasa-poo, and Eddie was a shih-a-poo—both very good dogs who lived to be sixteen and fifteen and a half. They were faithful friends who welcomed babies home and sat next to me through every breastfeeding.

I also tried to take walks, ask for help, and nap when my babies napped, but how did I do that with a newborn AND a toddler?? Well, all that teacher training and planning did not go to waste. I began to make lists and schedules, not only for my boys but also for myself. I picked days for laundry. I picked days for certain dinners. I picked days for outings, and I looked into preschool as soon as possible. Why? It not only gave me two hours, two days a week, with only one at home, but it also gave Hunter some time to learn things like social interaction and self-control. It was a blessing for me to refocus, even if just for an hour or two.

My mom and mother-in-love also were a big help. I was so thankful for their help on my journey, from helping with laundry to tag-teaming diapers; I felt a glimmer of hope that my whole life would not always be about diapers!

Remember I mentioned *Baby Wise* in the last chapter? Well, Chapter 11, titled "Parenting Potpourri: Topics of Interest to New Parents," mentions the playpen. Ah, the glorious and wonderful playpen—it is a very helpful tool to help your baby learn mental-focusing skills, attention span, creativity, order, and the ability to entertain himself or herself. It can be used as early as two months old when the "baby has alert waketimes for fifteen to thirty minutes."[2] So, I did this with all four of my boys, and it became a safe way to give myself a minute or two of calm or just time for my baby or toddler to learn some necessary skills for life. I gave them fun books, toys, etc., that would engage them, depending on how old they were. Be sure to consider using the playpen to help, especially if you have multiple children.

---

[2] Ezzo, Baby Wise, (p. 191).

Fast forward now about two years . . . it's now 2002, and Blake Daniel Chenevey entered this world on November 20. Now, I had three beautiful boys. Hunter was four years old, Luke was two and a half, Cole was seven, and Eddie was six (oh, and the dogs were males as well—forgot to mention that about the dynamics of my household, but you were probably smart, guessing they were boys based on their names. Lol!).

What everyone says is true—after you have two, one more is not really that different, except it really is. Ha ha! You have one more little life to keep alive and fed, but by now, you have a few rhythms established and more confidence than when you first brought home baby number one! I was that way, thanks to Jesus and the *BabyWise* books. It also helped that Hunter was finally potty-trained (not till age three!), and Luke was going to start learning, although not the month Blake was born. I do not recommend trying to potty train a two-and-a-half-year-old when you are about to give birth. Just sayin'.

Two in diapers didn't last as long as the Hunter and Luke era since Luke was a whole year older than Hunter was when Blake was born. But life became interesting when Jeff began to travel to Huntsville, Alabama. Maybe we will save that for the next chapter when I talk more about toddler years as well as our move to another state—and the birth of baby number four!!

CHAPTER 4 QUESTIONS

What does Isaiah 40:11 say that can be a comfort to moms with young babies?

James 1:3 is a great verse about what? Write it down here, and then say it out loud. Remember, it's good to allow your spirit to hear the Word of God. It helps feed and strengthen your spirit.

What are some ways you can help yourself to juggle and navigate everyday life as a mama? (HINT: What are some things I did that helped?)

Chapter 5

Three Boys and Counting

Life on the Mooooove!!

But they who wait on the LORD shall renew their strength;
they shall mount up with wings like eagles; they shall run
and not be weary; they shall walk and not faint.
—Isaiah 40:31

♪ DANCE PAUSE 🎵
"Break My Stride," Matthew Wilder

T he final box was taped and shut. Our movers pulled away from our home in Medina, Ohio, and I felt a lump in my throat. I remember the skies were rainy, often found here in Northeast Ohio, as our "new" good friends, Tracy and Bill, came over to say goodbye. Bill showed Jeff his new car and took him for a ride while Tracy and I "got deep" in the kitchen of our empty home. We bravely smiled and said we would stay in touch. She had quickly become one of my best friends, often giggling about everyday things and talking about how to be more like Jesus as wives and moms. She was a rare treasure to me, so I embraced her and cried that I would stay in touch. We grabbed the kids and pups and dragged ourselves into our two cars. My mom and Jeff's parents joined us in a caravan to our new "promised land" in Madison, Alabama. But we, too, had to wander through the desert first.

The definition of a desert, according to the Oxford Dictionary, is "a dry, barren area of land . . . characteristically desolate, waterless, and without vegetation." And isn't it funny that if you pronounce it differently, it can mean to "abandon or leave a place empty"? Interesting . . . and just one more "s," and the whole word changes!! It becomes dessert—mmmmmm, yummy! So, let's unpack what we can learn from this word and the desert experience God sometimes allows us to walk through (and notice how I said "through"—we don't stay there; we need to keep going because the desert is not where we are supposed to stay).

Jesus spent forty days and forty nights in the desert, fasting and praying, right after He was baptized by His cousin John (Matthew chapters 3 and 4). The devil came and tried to tempt Him three times, and each time, Jesus mic-dropped the devil with what the Word of God said and then told him to get lost! The devil departed, and Scripture says, "Angels came and took care of Jesus" (Matthew 4:11). Why the desert? What big thing happened after Jesus was in the desert? And what do you think was the plan for Jesus to be in the desert for so long?

_____

_____

_____

_____

_____

Thanks for pausing and thinking about these questions. As you do, it will help you gain what the Lord would have you learn here.

Jesus went on to begin His ministry at age thirty, which lasted for three years! So, the desert experience was designed to be His final prep for the big "thing" God had for His Son.

Maybe you are in a desert. Maybe you have been in one way too long, and you're wondering what is going on. Let me tell you—it's important to learn what you can in the desert. It's important for your gettin-out-of-the-desert-sooner for you to embrace the lesson. When we resist and complain, well, you know what happened to the Israelites, right? Yeah, forty years in the desert, and many did not even make it to the Promised Land! Let's not have that happen to you. Let's see what we might be able to learn in the desert.

The devil tried to tempt Jesus to turn stone into bread, to jump off a high point, and to worship him. Jesus' response was the sword of the Spirit, the Word of God. He said, "People do not live by bread alone, but by every word that comes from the mouth of God." On the second try, Jesus responded with, "The Scriptures also say, 'You must not test the LORD your God.'" And finally, He tells the devil to leave because the Word says, "You must worship the LORD your God and serve only him" (Matthew 4:1–11, NLT). Jesus is our example. He showed us here that we should remember to stay in the Word, not to test the Lord, and to worship and serve only Jesus.

Our desert experiences where we feel alone, lost, overlooked, mistreated, tempted, confused, forgotten, and misguided are times for us to press into the Word of God and refocus on where we are going, what we are learning, and what God is speaking to us because you know what comes next? The Promised Land!! Yes, and we get to go to our promised land, our next assignment, where we can be used mightily if we allow Jesus to work in us while we are in the desert. So, moving away to Alabama felt a little like a desert.

(God Pause!)

Are you in a desert right now? If not now, can you explain a desert-like time you had? What did you learn from that time? What are you learning now?

But the blessing in being in Alabama was that now our whole family would be together. Although we were forging a whole new life in a totally different place (that was VERY HOT—so it was like a desert!), we found joy in seeing "Daddy" every day as well as going to the apartment complex pool! We all packed into an apartment for nine weeks. Yes, all five of us and two dogs went from a three-bedroom house to a three-bedroom apartment! Why did we do this? Well, we had this cool house we were building, so it was worth the wait. And it was! It was especially worth it the day Blake said "Daddy" for the first time.

When we moved to Alabama, Blake was eighteen months old, and during the first year and a half of his life, Jeff was traveling to Huntsville, Alabama, every week, Monday through Thursday. It was a very busy and exhausting time for all of us. We did our best to keep things family-focused and happy, but sometimes it was not fun. We knew we had to make some decisions, and, therefore, the move to Alabama. We decided it would be an adventure, and Jeff also had some great opportunities with his job if we moved.

Little did we know that Hayden Michael Chenevey would be born during our visit to the "desert" of Alabama. Yes, after being in Alabama for about a year, I found out I was pregnant. I had weathered a year of getting to know the lay of the land, finding favorite stores and eateries, finding doctors, the dentist, and hair salons—you know, all the important stuff. It was rather exhausting! But I pressed on thinking, *I need to walk through the desert, not stay here.* I found a great program called Mother's Morning Out for Blake, and Hunter and Luke attended Little Madison Academy that first year. I looked into a MOPS (Mothers of Preschoolers), a group that I had belonged to in Ohio, and I found another mom's group that played Bunco. Also, we attended one church and enrolled the kids in Awana at another church closer to our home. I found this church the first summer we were there when I took the boys to one Vacation Bible School event after another, and then I ended up in a wonderful ladies' Bible study with lots of other moms. When you seek these things, the Lord surely provides!

I kept them on the go, and I knew my extroverted self needed to connect. I also hit the jackpot when a new friend told me about a scrapbooking group that had retreats several times a year at a place in the country where the owners made all three meals for the scrapbookers—and the meals were all homemade! I would sign up right away for these retreats, and they became my "saving grace" in the desert—or maybe more aptly named, my oasis. I would leave and spend two to three nights just enjoying creating and remembering as I made new friends and was just Renee for a little bit again. Be sure to take time to discover things that bring you joy and make time to do them.

Why do I tell you all this? Well, I was establishing some new rhythms not only for my kids but for myself. It was healthy for me to have community, and I often did that with my kids. I also needed time away to recharge and refocus—sometimes, the desert can make us thirsty, and we need to make time to rehydrate.

(God Pause)

Rehydrate. I like that. How do you "rehydrate" your life when you become parched and dry? What rhythms do you have in place to help you balance each day so you don't get burned out, Mama? Do you have some things you really enjoy that aren't "work" to you? Take some time to "breathe" right now and think about these questions.

Ah, nice! Glad you took the time to think about what you enjoy. Think of those as the things that "rehydrate" you. When you are dehydrated, you become tired and uncomfortable and the same with being a mama. You will be a better wife and mama if you take time for you.

I'm glad I had some of these things in place when I found out baby number four was coming, but in the midst of all this, Jeff's job was in question . . .

Yeah, we moved to Alabama for a contract that was supposed to last four years, but a year into it, things changed. It was a government contract with NASA, and as I understood these contracts, sometimes things changed in the government budget, and then contracts changed. Jeff found himself traveling again while I held down the fort in the desert and became bigger and bigger physically (with a baby, of course—stop judging!).

We prayed and knew God hadn't brought us this far to leave us in the desert, let alone be separated in the desert. We stood in faith for the things we hoped for (Hebrews 11:1) and agreed to trust the Lord for the right open door.

I remember the day . . . I was about eight months pregnant and on our stationary bike in our "bonus" room when Jeff walked upstairs and peeked through the door. His face was hard to read. I couldn't tell if it was shock or sadness, but I stopped pedaling; pregnancy pounds would have to wait.

"Renee," he said and stared at me. I stared back, my heart racing. "I just got done talking to Chuck (his boss), and he was able to negotiate to get me back here at NASA to work!" I started to cry, knowing Jesus had come through just in time. I was going to have my hubby home when Hayden Michael made his out-of-womb appearance! God is so good.

Sure enough, on December 17, 2005, Hayden Michael Chenevey was born nine days early in Huntsville, Alabama. He was a healthy guy, weighing in at eight pounds, one ounce and twenty-one inches long. The rest of the crew came with Dad a little later, and my mom jumped in her car and drove twelve hours to help tag team the whirlwind I was about to enter. It was a fun Christmas enjoying life being together and knowing our prayers had been answered.

CHAPTER 5 QUESTIONS

Why did Jesus spend forty days and forty nights in the desert? What is your understanding of why we have desert experiences in our lives?

What were the three ways the devil tried to tempt Jesus, and how did Jesus respond? How should we respond to temptations while we are in the desert?

What did I do to reinvent myself in this season of moving to help myself be healthy? What can you learn from my experience to apply to your life?

See you in Chapter 6! Don't worry—no more babies coming. Let's see how I navigated being a mom in the toddler years.

Chapter 6

Toddler Years—
Tips and Trials

Living Life in the Alabama
Desert with Four Boys

It's ready, set, go, it's another wild day
When the stress is on the rise in my heart, I feel you say
Just breathe, just breathe
Come and rest at my feet, And be, just be
Chaos calls, but all you really need
Is to just breathe (breathe, breathe, breathe).
"Breathe," music and lyrics by Jonny Diaz, 2015

♪ DANCE PAUSE ♫
"Breathe," Jonny Diaz

B reathe. Hmmm . . . not something we all tend to really think about, right? But sometimes, it's exactly what we need. I remember when this song came out in 2015, many years after living in the Alabama desert, but it's appropriate for what my life felt like during this time and many, many years of my deep-in-the-trenches mommyhood. If you get a chance, look up this awesome song. The lyrics are just great. Jonny Diaz describes the chaos of parenting in words like "alarm clock screaming bare feet hit the floor . . . It's off to the races, everybody out the door." Feel like you are rushing, rushing, rushing? Or maybe you are in the take-a-nap-with-baby over and over. Either way, you understand the difficulty of doing "normal" things—like getting out the door—now has become quite an Olympic feat! Lots of planning goes into getting out the door with all your babies—the night before is, "Did I sign that paper? Do you have your lunch money? Who is doing your carpool today? Did you brush your teeth? Did you use soap when you washed?"

So, let's practice right now. Breathe. Breathe in . . . breathe out. Is your list so long that you can't see the end? Well, lay that all down right now. Write down what you need to do right here—yes, all of it. Get it out of your head so you can focus on this next thing I will have you do.

My list of things in my head . . .

_____

_____

_____

_____

_____

Now, I have this cool Apple Watch that sometimes reminds me to breathe. Isn't that funny? "Don't forget to breathe" is a little odd, but I will tell you a story about how I actually held my breath in a role-playing illustration when I went on a reflective retreat called "Making Peace with My Past," written and sponsored by my counselor at the time, Jamie Norton.

Here's what happened: I had been seeing Jamie for about a year when she asked me about a weekend she was having. It was an opportunity to look at things in my past that may be weighing me down. She called on me, and I was a little apprehensive. There were about twenty-five other people at the event. She asked me to begin listing things in my life that needed and wanted my time. I quickly named my husband and my children, my dogs, my extended family, church responsibilities, exercise, food planning, appointments—anyway, you get the idea. I had to be very specific. She wrote everything on a wipe board that everyone could see.

Then, she went around the room and assigned each person one of the "things" vying for my time. Next, she put me in the middle of a circle they all made around me. She asked each person to be that thing in my life and say out loud what that may sound like in my life:

> *I need you, Mommy!*
> *Can you follow up with the plumber who came, Hon?*
> *Where's my stuff for football, Mama?*
> *Woof! I'm hungry!*
> *We need to plan a party for Mom for her seventieth, Renee.*
> *Can you volunteer for the nursery this Sunday?*
> *Mama, we need a physical for track—due next week.*

I don't remember how long it lasted, but it was long enough to impact me to this day. Jamie stopped everyone and put her hands on me. She said, "Renee, you stopped breathing. I could tell that you held your breath." She proceeded to unpack what this meant, and as she did, I broke down in tears. That wasn't the end. After I recovered, she explained to me that I needed better boundaries in my life. She had me say to each thing in my life the following: "I am willing to _____, but I am not willing to _____."

For example, I remember telling the person being Hunter, my oldest, that I was willing to allow him to help me where I needed it, but I was not willing to let him take on so much responsibility that he didn't get to be a kid. Good, huh? I did this with EVERYTHING that surrounded me. Wow. All I can say is—wow.

What do you take on that you don't need to, Mama? What are you carrying that only Jesus can? You are not responsible for the happiness of everyone around you either. That's not your job. Your job is to be a caregiver to your kids, to guide them in the things of Jesus, but you are not their Savior.

Let's take a minute right now to look at YOUR list and maybe add a few things that want and need your attention. Then, think about what boundary you might need to make with each thing/person.

"I am willing to _____, but I am not willing to _____."

Another example would be, "I am willing to volunteer at church, but I am not going to feel like I have to say yes to everything. I know I need to be prayerful in all my decisions before I say yes."

Maybe do this in your own journal. Take as long as you need, but this exercise would have helped me so much if I had known about it ten years before I actually did. So, I want you, Mama, to be healthy in your walk of mommyhood. Some of my stress could have been avoided if I had learned to breathe and have firmer boundaries. You can do it! It will be worth spending the time to think about it.

So, boundaries are not only good for you but are especially good for toddlers. Let's get back to those four precious boys of mine and what I did with them in the Alabama desert.

One of the greatest things I did was continue to change and adapt my children's structure to their days, depending on each of their respective ages. Hayden and Blake's day had a little different look than the day for Hunter and Luke at this point. Blake was almost there, being that he was now three. At least at this stage of the game, I only had ONE in diapers. Thank the Lord!! I didn't spend time here in this book discussing potty training, but you could message me, and I can tell you more about that personally.

Remember the book I told you about called *On Becoming Baby Wise?* Well, the same authors wrote many other books for each stage of development. The second one is called *On Becoming Toddler Wise,* for parenting the second year from first steps to potty training. The premise of this book talks a lot about boundaries to have depending on the age of a child. A two-year-old will not have as many freedoms, obviously, as a twelve-year-old. As a child grows and has better self-control and comprehension of the world, the more the child can have freedoms. I like how Gary Ezzo and Dr. Robert Bucknam describe the result of giving too little or too much freedom to a child who doesn't understand or who doesn't have the right amount of self-control:

1. Freedoms greater than self-control = developmental confusion
2. Freedoms less than self-control = developmental frustration
3. Freedoms equal self-control = developmental harmony[3]

So, they explain, "When naughtiness abounds more than self-control, and when defiance overpowers compliance," you may want to evaluate if you have given your child too many freedoms too early.[4] Over time, your child will move from their playpen to their room to the backyard, but doing this too soon is not only dangerous to your child physically but is also dangerous to their mental and emotional decisions and overall attitude with you.

Having this understanding, let's look at how I structured my boys' days as they grew. We talked about the playpen, but there's also room time and some other things. A routine was my lifesaver, but I also had to learn that this routine sometimes would not be exactly as I would like. I had to learn to be flexible so that when some unexpected stuff happened, I didn't get all

---

[3] Robert Bucknam, MD, and Gary Ezzo, On Becoming Toddler Wise: From First Steps to Potty Training (Parentwise Solutions, 2003), 36.

[4] Bucknam and Ezzo, Toddler Wise, 37.

crazy-mama. But without some structure and routine, I was leaving it all to chance, and that's not good either.

First of all, you, as the mama, set the bedtime and when the day starts. Keep this for years, and you will not regret it! Make this consistent. Teach your toddler to wait for you and not to wander the house till you come to them in the morning (this is before potty training, so no worries on potty time). After eating breakfast, what does their day look like? Ideas would be room time, free playtime, structured playtime, structured playtime with siblings, playtime with Mommy, playtime with friends, and video/TV time (this is helpful around preparing for dinner!).

The afternoon might look like lunch, nap time, room time, structured playtime with Mommy or siblings, and then video/TV time. And then, evening would begin with dinner, family time, Dad's time with kids, and couch time (remember this? It's for Mom and Dad—and good for kids to see you making each other a priority). Bath time is next and then bedtime is last. Have a routine for bedtime . . . reading together, praying, etc.[5] Maybe play soft music to help them settle down, but whatever you do, try to have a routine. Kids with routines are more settled and become more confident as they get older.

Another area to discuss would be correction. Having boundaries means some more strong-willed kiddos will push the limit, and what will you do? Does the Bible say anything about this? Why, yes, it does. So glad you asked! But let's take a minute to review before we move on.

What are some things you want your child to do in a day? Jot down some thoughts here . . . and if you don't have any kind of routine or schedule, maybe start small with one of your ideas and go from there. But consider your toddler needs rest (and so do you!).

---

[5] Bucknam and Ezzo, Toddler Wise, 48–56.

_____

_____

_____

_____

_____

Okay, good! Now, take some time after you finish this chapter to come up with a schedule you actually write out. This way, you are more likely to follow it.

The Bible says, "Train up a child in the way he should go, and when he is old he will not depart from it" (Proverbs 22:6, NKJV). And Proverbs 15:32 says, "Those who disregard discipline despise themselves, but the one who heeds correction gains understanding" (NIV). As parents, we have a responsibility to train, guide, and correct our children so when they are older, they have understanding and know how to live lives that honor Jesus. But it doesn't just happen. We begin with prayer, and then we use age-appropriate correction. Because our sweet, beautiful babies are guaranteed not to always be sweet and perfect 24/7, how will we respond if we don't really know how we want to respond or what will be effective?

Let's start with the recommended principles of instruction from Ezzo and Bucknam, still in their *Toddler Wise* book. These principles will set the foundation for all you do in correction and parenting. If you can do these things now, it will really save you from greater heartache in the future. I can give testimony to this! Granted, each child is different and may require more "review" moments, but ALL children can be helped to reach higher standards, and in reality, this is what the Lord requires of us. He wants us to exhibit the fruit of the Spirit in our lives, and one way is also teaching our children what that looks like too.

The four principles are the following:

1. When you speak to your child in a way that requires an answer or an action, you should expect a response. An exploring toddler is in the process of learning, so remember he will not be capable of obedience 100 percent of the time.

2. With toddlers, you must give instructions, not suggestions. You are the mama, so don't ask your eighteen-month-old if she wants to go to bed!!

3. Healthy discipline is always consistent. Draw the line and stay with it. Consistency provides security and freedom, and it also helps them learn moral orderliness in the world—some behaviors will result in punishment or consequences, and others will be followed by praise and encouragement.

4. Require eye contact when giving face-to-face instructions. This actually helps your child focus and better process each instruction. By sixteen to eighteen months, you can require a "yes, Mommy" after an instruction.[6]

Isn't this great?! Writing this now and seeing the proven result with my own boys is so exciting. So, I tell you these things because I know it works. More times than I can count, I would have complete strangers say, "Wow, your kids are so well-behaved." It's the godly wisdom of Jesus, as well as these two men imparting what God gave them, that helped that happen. I just had to be obedient to carry it out consistently.

Okay, last thing: What are some age-appropriate corrections at the toddler stage? Yes, you heard of the terrible twos? Well, I am here to lessen that fear and help you, Mama, have more control and hope for what you can do to guide and correct your self-absorbed—although so, so cute—toddler!

[6] Ezzo and Bucknam, Toddler Wise, 94–96.

Here are the options for correction from Ezzo and Bucknam in *Toddler Wise*:

- *Redirecting*—Help redirect your child's attention from what they are doing, which may be wrong, dangerous, or unwise, to a new activity.

- *Isolation*—Children are social by nature, so isolation temporarily takes away the privilege of social contact. At home, isolate the child to the crib, bed, or chair. Screaming and temper-tantrum kids, be sure to isolate in the crib or bed. Once they are calm and happy, isolation ends.

- *Natural consequences*—A mischievous toddler's actions will sometimes have natural consequences. For example, Mama says STOP but the child doesn't, and he runs into a wall. This natural consequence will teach your kiddo for the future.

- *Loss of privilege*—Child loses right to play with toy or friend because of misbehavior.

- *Nap time*—Sometimes, the root cause of misbehavior is tiredness. Temper tantrums are often a result of an overstimulated child who needs sleep.

- *Other*—This is for whatever works for you and your family value system. Remember to use this with grace and love.[7]

Phew! That was a lot in one chapter, but I really hope you see the value in my telling you all this. With four active boys, I found myself needing to have a plan. In the next chapter, I will talk more about the principles of raising kids ages three to seven. For now, let's take time to answer some questions to help you remember all these valuable morsels of information.

---

[7] Ezzo and Bucknam, *Toddler Wise*, 102–103.

CHAPTER 6 QUESTIONS

What is the sentence you can say when trying to set boundaries in your own life as a mama so you stay balanced and healthy?

Tell me about what too much freedom can cause. What does a child need to have more freedoms?

Jot down one of the two verses I mentioned regarding what the Bible says about discipline.

What are the four principles of instruction for training your child?

What are some of the options for correction when disciplining and training your toddler?

Chapter 7

Preschool Training and Tips

Dancing in the Desert with Four Boys

You have turned for me my mourning into dancing; you
have loosed my sackcloth and clothed me with gladness, that
my glory may sing your praise and not be silent.
—*Psalm 30:11–12*

♪ DANCE PAUSE ♫
"I Feel Like Dancing," Jason Mraz

D ancing in the desert? That doesn't sound like a lot of fun, right? But I do know this is the dry kind of heat—you know, not the other kind of heat that means lots of humidity. So maybe that's better. I've been to Arizona, and hot is hot to me, but having been out of the country, I now know humidity is a lot worse. It's heat that feels like you can't breathe. And breathing is important for life and living.

Dancing has always been something I love. I was never a "trained" dancer, but I always had a good rhythm and could do cheerleading dances every year pretty well. And, of course, I always loved a good wedding for dancing with people you most likely won't see again, and if you do, you can just blame it on the celebration getting the best of you. Ha ha! But seriously, something I always liked to do with my boys was a little dance fest. Sometimes, I would just put on the radio or play a tape cassette we made, but usually, we did this when we all needed time to burn off some energy and have some fun together. I recommend it tremendously! We always found ourselves laughing and giggling and, at the same time, getting some exercise. Bonus! Later, when we moved out of the "desert," we often did Michael Jackson's Wii Experience, and it became a competition to see who could nail the moves the best.

So find something you can do with your kids all together while you might be in a season where you need some joy. We always found it in music and exercising together this way, and during the preschool and elementary years, this was a common occurrence that I have not once regretted making time for with my boys.

(God Pause)

Let's take a minute and brainstorm some ideas of things you could do with your kids to have fun and burn some calories at the same time.

Okay, great, now you can implement your ideas into your daily routine. Refer back to Chapter 6, if needed, about creating a routine and why.

Back to the desert . . .

Even though I was far from home, the Lord gave me an oasis that helped sustain me in many ways. I continued to utilize Mother's Morning Out for preschool for my younger boys, and Hunter and Luke attended Little Madison Academy for kindergarten and later Columbia Elementary for first through third grades. I found still having my routine with my younger boys helped me be more attentive when Hunter and Luke came home from school. I would then always have them decompress with a good snack and some fun cartoon or TV show. Sometimes, they wanted to get right at their homework, but I always told them it was good to get some food in their bellies and a little laugh in their spirit before tackling it all. After about thirty minutes, we would talk a little and then head to the table in our dining room to go through what was needed for that night's homework. Often, that included reading time as well for about twenty minutes, which worked great for the younger two also. But again, we always followed a routine, which not only helped my boys feel secure but also kept me calmer and focused. This helped give my boys a peace, I truly believe, that has been a foundation for them as they have grown up.

This same principle applies to the impact of the marriage relationship on your kids. If you are a single mom, remember the Lord is a Redeemer, and He also promises to give the peace and stability needed to your children, whether it's through providing a male role model at church or another family member. Just trust the Lord to provide.

Gary Ezzo and Robert Bucknam emphasize that a basic need of a child is "to know his/her world is stable."[8] A child needs to know his parents care for and love each other, and this "radar" is in tune at this preschool age as early as three years old.[9] Therefore, creating routines first establishes this security, and then it's reinforced by the family dynamics of mom and dad

---

[8] Gary Ezzo and Robert Bucknam, MD, On Becoming Child Wise: Parenting Your Child from Three to Seven Years (Parent Wise Solutions, Inc., 2001), 39.

[9] Ezzo and Bucknam, Child Wise, 39.

interactions. So, as a reminder from earlier chapters, don't forget couch time. And, Mama, if you are single, have your time with the Lord on a couch out in the open and remind your child that you are spending time with Jesus. It will have a similar impact on your child. As the Bible says, "For your Maker is your husband. The LORD of hosts is His name; and your Redeemer is the Holy One of Israel; He is called the God of the whole earth" (Isaiah 54:5–8, NKJV). It's amazing how the Lord thinks of everything, and He knows that the world is broken. But He promises to meet our needs in a way that is best for us.

Some other principles are presented in this third book of the *BabyWise* series, *On Becoming Child Wise*. This book covers parenting your child from ages three to seven, so this will get us to the point where we will be ready for the elementary years. The main principles are worth mentioning here so that your mindset can stay balanced and healthy as you move forward in your parenting and as your child grows. Two main principles are that you will "use the strength of your leadership early on and the strength of your relationship later on," as well as "parent now, be friends later."[10] Your leadership is so important as your child navigates life up till about age ten, and then your relational influence will be more important. What does this mean exactly? Your leadership will be more about compliance and conformity at first, and then you need to allow your child room to make sound decisions and gain confidence as they mature and get older. This will be important for their healthy growth as they move into the teen years.

Ezzo and Bucknam mention four phases of parenting that I think are also worth mentioning here. Keep these phases tucked away in your thoughts as you move forward with your child. The first phase is Leadership, which covers ages two to six years of age, with your main goal being to establish your leadership. The second is Training, for ages seven to twelve, where, like an athlete in training, you may stop at times for correction along the way. The third, Coaching, is the phase from ages thirteen to nineteen where your child is now on their own, and you can give them tips from the

---

[10] Ezzo and Bucknam, *Child Wise*, 50, 54.

sidelines—but you can't stop the game and show them how to do it. Finally, phase four is Friendship, when you find yourself in a new relationship with your kids where you are "morally and relationally netted together in your hearts."[11] Isn't this just great? I can attest that the friendship phase is just so wonderful. It was worth every battle and every prayer and every teaching moment. So stay the course now, and you will reap the benefits later. That reminds me of the verse in Galatians 6 that says:

> *Do not be deceived: God is not mocked, for whatever one sows,*
> *that will he also reap. For the one who sows to his own flesh will*
> *from the flesh reap corruption, but the one who sows to the Spirit*
> *will from the Spirit reap eternal life. And let us not grow weary in*
> *doing good, for in due season we will reap, if we do not*
> *give up (verses 7–9).*

What you plant in your kids now will allow you to harvest a great friendship later in life. Don't miss this principle. Don't try to be friends when your kids are young and need your leadership. Follow these suggestions above regarding the phases of parenting, and you won't be disappointed.

Phew! That's a lot. How are you feeling? These are super important foundations you can establish in your child's early years, and, speaking from a mama who has three of her four kids in this phase, it does work! I have friendships with my sons now, and they are healthy and thriving as adults.

So dancing in the desert looks a little like embracing the gifts your children are. It looks like embracing moments to make memories; it looks intentional, prayer-covered, and orderly. It is all the good and all the bad but taking time each day to evaluate how it's going. What's working and what's not? And as you evaluate, think of some of the principles that I have mentioned throughout these seven chapters. What needs tweaking? What behaviors do you see in your child that are not favorable? Why might he be acting this way? It is always good to take time to be aware, to evaluate, to

---

[11] Ezzo and Bucknam, *Child Wise*, 55–57.

discern what is going on in your child's heart and mind. If you take the time now, you will find your child grows into a healthy, confident, and independent adult who can freely use the gifts God has given them to impact the world. And isn't that what we were commissioned to do as parents? We raise our children up so they can move and live and breathe all that God has for them, and, therefore, they can glorify God with their lives.

Well, I think it might be almost time to leave the Alabama desert. As we have learned to rehydrate here and dance in the heat of the trials, we have also learned to embrace the season the Lord has us in. As we embrace and learn, we can then move into a new season where we have new adventures and opportunities to learn and grow.

The next chapter will be mostly about the things I did during these years to keep myself healthy. It will be a little diversion from going in order of my kids' development, but it will be a good opportunity to really evaluate the way I redefined myself as I moved from only Renee to wife to Mommy. Before we do that, let's answer some questions.

CHAPTER 7 QUESTIONS

What are some ways to have fun with your kids? What are you implementing now? (Maybe share some ideas on my Facebook page with other mamas.)

What is a basic need of a child? How can this need be met through the mom and dad?

What are the four phases of parenting? Why is it important to consider these phases and adhere to them?

Fill in the blank: . . . for whatever one _____ that will he also reap. For the one who sows to his own _____, will from the _____ reap_____, but the one who sows from the _____ will from the _____ reap _____life. And let us not grow_____ in doing good, for in due season we will reap, if we do not give up (Galatians 6:7–9).

Chapter 8

Who Am I Now?

How I Redefined Myself through the Desert

I see you, child, though you can't see me
And I know your thoughts before you even think
I heard every last prayer you prayed though I answered all the time
You just didn't hear my reply.
And I know it's not easy, oh, don't you give up on me
Don't you give up on me cause the darker the night gets
The brighter the light hits
Child, we're just getting started; open your heart, open your hands
Open your eyelids; I've got more dreams
I've got more plans, I've got more blessings
Don't lose your hope, Don't lose your faith
I've got more dreams . . . more plans . . . more blessings
There is so much more, so much, so much, so much more
"Don't Give Up on Me," lyrics and music by Brandon Lake, 2022

♪ DANCE PAUSE 🎵
"Don't Give Up on Me," Brandon Lake

Okay, so as you can see, I chose to quote a lot of a recent song that really spoke to me as I was ready to sit down and write this chapter. I suggest right now for you to stop and find a way to listen to this Brandon Lake song. You can click on the QR code above, grab your AirPods, headphones, or whatever you have, and take a minute (well, the song is four and a half minutes, but you get the idea). What are you waiting for? Go! Go! Go! See you back here in about five minutes.

Five minutes later . . .

Do you feel unseen? Are you pouring out every day? Maybe you are working AND being Mama and all that entails. Maybe you are the kind of personality that gives 110 percent, and you feel lost a little. Maybe you had your babies, and you love it so much you have made them the center of your life. Maybe God and your husband are standing on the sidelines waiting to be seen by you, or you are wondering why you feel sad at times. Have you forgotten about you? Have you pushed aside all the things you enjoy to meet everyone's needs around you?

You may be struggling with these thoughts or maybe already dealt with them, and now you find yourself as an empty nester, not knowing who you are anymore. My friend, we are all at different stages reading this book but don't underestimate the Lord's power to time this just for you and where you are right now. The lyrics in this song say, "I see you, Child . . . I've got more dreams, I've got more plans, I've got more blessings . . . there is so much more. We're just getting started!"

That is exciting. New mom, seasoned mom, empty nester, grandma—you are still here, so God still has things for you to do. The Bible says not to look back at former things because then you miss what God has for you right in front of you. We often expect our lives to stay the same from year to year, and, in reality, many of us like what's comfortable, right? We don't really like to have change. Change can be painful, and that's not fun. But in our pain, we grow—if we yield to its benefits. Yes, I said pain can be beneficial—not fun, but beneficial. So let's unpack those two thoughts—not looking back and the benefits of pain. Philippians 3:13–14 says:

Brothers and sisters, I do not consider myself yet to have taken hold of it. But one thing I do: Forgetting what is behind and straining toward what is ahead, I press on toward the goal to win the prize for which God has called me heavenward in Christ Jesus (NIV).

Forget the former things; do not dwell on the past. See, I am doing a new thing! Now it springs up; do you not perceive it? I am making a way in the wilderness and streams in the wasteland (Isaiah 43:18–19, NIV).

I love how the Old and New Testaments tie themes together. We are told to leave what's behind, to keep our focus on what God has for us not only eternally but also on how He makes a way in the wilderness. He is always doing a new thing in us, so we can't keep thinking who we were before kids is who we are to be now. We are always growing and trying to be more like Jesus. We can't do that if we are always longing to "go back to Egypt." Maybe there were three full meals a day there, but the Lord wants us to do something more than just give us the basics. He still has more for us.

Our desert experience doesn't last even if we have gotten used to it; we have a promised land we need to get to that might involve some uncomfortable change, but it will be worth it. We wouldn't change being mamas for the world, but sometimes, many of our own dreams are lost as we sacrifice to be wholly present with our kids and point them to Jesus. And sometimes, we struggle and have pain and feel so tired we can barely lift up that cup of coffee.

Romans 5:3–5 says:

But we also glory in our sufferings, because we know that suffering produces perseverance; perseverance, character; and character, hope. And hope does not put us to shame, because God's love has been poured out into our hearts through the Holy Spirit, who has been given to us (NIV).

And 1 Peter 1:6–7 helps us know that trials prove our faith genuine:

In all this you greatly rejoice, though now for a little while you may have had to suffer grief in all kinds of trials. These have come so that the proven genuineness of your faith—of greater worth than gold, which perishes even though refined by fire—may result in praise, glory and honor when Jesus Christ is revealed (NIV).

(God Pause)

What is produced in our suffering (this can just be as simple as change)? Look at these verses and jot down what you believe God is saying about pain.

Okay, good—you see this reminder that our suffering produces perseverance, character, hope, and the genuineness of our faith! Now, I'm not saying we will always be skipping around and praising the Lord for how much we love our pain, but I am saying not to ignore it. Don't run away from it or hide in things that can harm you.

Can I share some things I did to rediscover myself and stay healthy through various seasons of mommyhood? Why, thank you! Please don't close the book at this point. This is a super-duper important chapter. I will allude to other ways I have navigated life as the lives of my kids changed, but this chapter is a summary of what I did up to this point.

Jumping into babyhood, I found myself with a lot of time on my own when Hunter was sleeping. I found some things I enjoyed and challenged my mind. As funny as it may seem, I played a Nintendo game. I would read a book about the game that had hints and places to record victories. I know it may seem a little weird, but it was so fun! I don't find as much joy in that now, but wow, it was awesome back then! Lol! I needed something to "achieve" for my brain, and this was something that met that need. I also found time to take walks and exercise, as well as go to Bible studies that offered childcare. I was a new woman after just an hour or two of not having to keep another human alive 24/7.

So, in this early stage, what did I do? Well, I like to think of the verse about how Jesus grew "in wisdom and stature, and in favor with God and man" (Luke 2:52, NIV). He was our example of a balanced life. This verse talks of our growing mentally, physically, spiritually, and socially. As mamas, we often are spent physically right after our precious one comes out of the womb, but we often are spent in all these other areas too. God promises to give us strength when we are weak, and He carries us through the "boot camp" of parenthood. But when the dust settles, it's good to start attending to each of these areas a little at a time. I would say be sure to start with your physical and spiritual. Be sure to nap when you can and take time to listen to worship music and pray while doing dishes or laundry. Your quiet time will look different than before babies but find ways to be sure your spirit is fed each day. It will help greatly with your spirit and outlook on all things. Next, try to fit in ten to fifteen minutes of physical exercise. Maybe take a walk with your baby in the stroller, or just play a little bit of music as you walk around the house or up and down the stairs. Eventually, plan time each day of at least thirty minutes to do something to help your body stay strong and keep things moving. These were the top two things I made sure I did each day.

As for the mental and social aspects, this came with church attendance and reading a book I enjoyed, as well as attending a Bible study when I felt more like my baby and I had a flexible routine.

As my boys entered preschool, I started to find some evenings to play Bunco or go to dinner with a friend. I also attended MOPS (Mothers of Preschoolers). This group was a lifesaver and also gave me the support I needed from other mamas in the same season as me. I also welcomed assistance from my family for help with watching the kids, so my husband and I could get away for a weekend or I could go to the store by myself.

How did all this happen? I had to be intentional, but I also made a routine for myself. Sunday became a day to think about the week, to plan groceries, meet with friends, or go on "field trips," church events, and date nights with my hubby. This helped greatly, as I needed to have a vision. I had to see how my life still had rhythm even though it had changed drastically from pre-parenting. But enjoying the season you are in is important. Embrace knowing, loving, and spending time with your kids, for as many say, and I can now, that time flies! So, while you are in it, it's important you are healthy in all the areas mentioned above. Being healthy helps you be the better you and the example to your kids.

Moving into kindergarten, I found having four kids took a lot of organizing. However, I had created a good foundation for myself and my family by this point. Things often ran like a "well-oiled machine." Always leave a margin for error and the unforeseen things that inevitably happen too. I had to learn this as part of being human and wanting to be sanctified. What do I mean by that? The ugly parts come out as we lose patience and feel tired or hungry, and through that, we learn our greater and greater dependence on God to guide and direct us. He gives the wisdom and direction we need in every season, but only if we allow it and surrender to it.

With the many schedules of four kids, I had to have a good calendar (before smartphones, I used a desk calendar and a wipe board—and I still use these as I am a very visual person!). Whatever works for you, have a plan for yourself and your family. It will help you stay sane and enjoy the order in the chaos.

Another way I rediscovered myself in each season was to be involved in my kids' classrooms and help with parties. This was a fun way to not only help my kids but also help other kids and the teachers. I would volunteer to help once a week in two of my kids' classrooms as well as find ways to go on field trips and help plan parties. Now, I wasn't the main room mom (I knew my limits!), but I was a helper. I always had to stop and think about what was too much each year before I volunteered.

I remember reading a great book that helped me with this called *The Best Yes* by Lysa Terkeurst. It was a great tool for deciding how to make decisions. For the Bible does say, "'I have the right to do anything,' you say—but not everything is beneficial. 'I have the right to do anything'—but not everything is constructive" (1 Corinthians 10:23, NIV). The Berean Standard Version says, "Everything is permissible but not everything is edifying." You may have two ministry decisions to make. Both options are permissible, but you have to ask yourself which one is more beneficial for the season you are in and for your family. Your "best yes" affects everyone around you, so take the time to be still before the Lord and wait for His response.

I remember when Hayden was about four, and I was missing teaching. I had hosted some Bible studies and enjoyed leading discussions, but I knew it was time to be stretched. I prayed about it and waited, and one day, my pastor's wife at the church we were attending approached me. I'll never forget her asking me about leading the women's ministry at the church, and something jumped in my spirit. It was exactly what I had heard from the Lord in my quiet time. It was amazing how the Lord confirmed my next step. It was a great opportunity for me to be stretched, to use my teaching background, and be able to minister to other women.

I not only redefined myself spiritually but I also was longing for a team sport experience again. It had been such a huge part of my life when I was younger. I began to search online for local teams, and I don't remember exactly how I found coed soccer, but I did. I began my journey in learning a sport I didn't really know super well; although I played a little club soccer in high school, I didn't grow up learning it. I was fast and athletic, so I caught on quickly and enjoyed getting to know some new friends while doing it. I not only played outdoor soccer but I also began to love indoor soccer even more. As the years passed and my body aged, I eventually knew this season was ending when my body took six months to heal from a pulled muscle! Nonetheless, it was a fun outlet for me for many, many years, and it was good I pursued it because it helped me physically, mentally, and socially.

So maybe think about things you enjoyed before kids. Is there something you would still enjoy now that would be beneficial to you? Maybe take a minute and jot down what might be coming to you in your thoughts. Think about things spiritually you might enjoy as well.

_____

_____

_____

_____

_____

Great job! Now, can I ask you to take some time this week to think about how to implement one new thing in one area of your life—spiritually, mentally, physically, or socially—that would be beneficial for you? Again, stop and pray before you jump in. Ask the Lord, "Is this my best YES for where I am right now and the season I am in?" Maybe take a few days till you feel a peace about it, but don't take too long because then you just might talk yourself out of it!

We are going to wrap up this pause in my story to continue on with where we left the Alabama desert and what God gave our family in our next promised land. I will continue to share how I navigated myself in some other creative ways as we continue on this journey.

I appreciate you and your willingness to walk and read your way through this book, and I promise you that as you invest some time in these pages, I have prayed for you and what God wants to reveal to you. So keep on keeping on, my friend, for God's not done with you (or this book) yet! (No questions for this chapter. Just keep praying about your best YES in all things.)

Chapter 9

Kindergarten and Elementary Years

Lessons Learned in the Desert and Beyond

My people will abide in a peaceful habitation, in
secure dwellings, and in quiet resting places.
—Isaiah 32:18

♪ DANCE PAUSE 🎵
"Home," Philip Phillips

W ho would have thought that I would be crying leaving the "desert"? I cried entering and cried leaving. Time in the desert taught me a resilience I didn't know I had, and it gave me a better dependence on the Lord and trusting His hand to direct ALL my steps, and not just the ones I preferred. Alabama became HOME. Although the roads were unfamiliar and unknown, I forged my way in confidence as the Lord went before me and opened new doors of friendship and new doors of stretching. Once again, fear tried to get the best of me, but on the other side of fear is a great adventure. So, Mama, push beyond your fears when things are unknown. Trust the One who created you and push forward into the unknown with strength and joy, for you know you are not alone—ever.

And that is exactly what I learned in the desert. I learned I am never alone. Whatever road the Lord leads me to, He will walk right beside me. He will walk right beside you. But you know, Mama, what would life be without adventure? Without change? Without growth? It would be quite still, boring, and flavorless. Yes, I said flavorless. You know when you eat a meal that has no spice, no fun for your tongue? Lol! I feel a scripture trying to find its way to this sentence . . . this page . . .

We are called to be "salt and light." Matthew 5:13 says:

> *You are the salt of the earth. But if the salt loses its*
> *saltiness, how can it be made salty again?*

And verse 14 and 15 go on to say:

> *You are the light of the world. A town built on a hill cannot be hidden.*
> *Neither do people light a lamp and put it under a bowl. Instead*
> *they put it on a stand, and it gives light to everyone in the house. In*
> *the same way, let your light shine before others, that they may see*
> *your good deeds and glorify your Father in heaven (NIV).*

No matter where you go and no matter what season you are in, God has a purpose and plan for your life. He will use you to encourage someone, pray for someone, and listen to someone. But if you just drift along the same path of sameness and comfort, you may never be moved enough to look around. Instead, your eyes will only be fixed on the same boring path you have been on for years.

Maybe that sounds harsh, but I just want to be real here. If we are called to be salt and light, we can't do that standing in a corner or only walking on our treadmill of life. Our eyes need to embrace a new scene, a new horizon, a new path He presents to us.

Moving to Alabama was difficult because we had to leave our family and all that was familiar to us. Lots of tears were shed, but in the yes, we knew God had given us His peace that this was the path we were to take.

So, in the desert, I found new and wonderful friendships. I found new spots that became my favorite places to eat or play and share with my boys. And, you know, in the desert, Hayden was born too! You just never know what God may bring to you in the desert. I also decided I wanted to learn the guitar. So I did, and I sang and did my first recital singing and playing the guitar! It's something I want to do again, but in that time frame, I embraced a new thing I wanted to learn. It kept me growing and enjoying life even while I felt like my purpose was not so significant. But of course, I was definitely significant to my husband and boys and, most of all, to God.

You are significant. You are salt. You are light. Rest in this truth. It's good and simple.

(God Pause)

How do you keep life salty? How are you a light right now? How might you need to get better at being a light to others? How can you simplify your life right now? What's one thing that might be weighing you down and keeping you from simplicity and saltiness?

Welcome back! During the last years of the desert experience, Hunter and Luke were moving along through kindergarten and elementary school. Blake was gearing up for kindergarten but was loving the Mother's Morning Out program at a local church. Hayden, however, was just two and a half when we moved, so he had some preschool experiences before heading "home" to Ohio. So let's talk about some things I did as a Mama during these years.

During the kindergarten and elementary years, life picked up speed. Hunter and Luke were trying out their skills in soccer and flag football, and then, eventually, tackle football. Plans had to be made to cook dinner, feed my army, and somehow get to practices on time. Making friends helped with this because then a carpool could be worked out, but it was very hard the first year as I was still connecting. I always remember my own mom saying, "This is why you have kids when you are young." What she meant is as I have aged over the many years of being a mama, I have found myself with less stamina. It's not bad for my age because I keep fit, exercising still and lifting weights. But I remember being able to go all day without too much of a problem, but now, phew, if I lay horizontal at 9:00 p.m., I am guaranteed a trip to never-never land! Ha ha!

During this same season, I decided to do a triathlon to get back in shape after having babies. I had never really thought about doing one until my husband suggested it. It was a good focus for me. I read all I could get my hands on and then made a plan for myself to reach my goals based on the date of the race. It was another opportunity to navigate who I was in this busy season, where many of my own dreams were put on hold. I had something to work toward to better myself physically and mentally and, in many ways, spiritually too. I did lots of praying the morning of the race!

Is there something you would like to try that you never have? What's stopping you? Time? Help? Ask other moms or family members if they would be willing to walk alongside you in a goal you have. You'd be surprised by the willingness of people to help you if you ask.

What season are you navigating right now as you read this? Is there something you would like to do or achieve that would bring you joy or refreshing? Take a minute to answer these two questions and meet me back here in a few minutes (or however long you need).

After practices each night, it was time for baths or showers. Then, we all came together and read the Bible and prayed every night. We sometimes talked about the day, and we had the older boys practice praying for us all on different nights. This routine helped set the stage every night so that everyone could get much-needed sleep. Sometimes, I wondered how I could keep juggling it all, but now I wonder where the time went and find myself reflecting on the joys of these simple but powerful memories with my boys.

Another factor that helped establish a team spirit during these years was to have Saturday chores. Blake and Hayden had very simple things, such as setting the table daily or putting toys away, but Hunter and Luke started to learn to clean a bathroom and vacuum their rooms. But no matter what age your kids are, you can teach them responsibility and teamwork. I was always right there with them doing "my chores" so they could see we all work together. This was a rhythm that lasted all through my boys' growing-up years. There was always a buzz of music and laughing, as well as questions of, "Who has the vacuum?" on these Saturday mornings. It's a buzz I no longer hear anymore, but that's okay (I can say that now after shedding a few tears after writing this right now). I grieve some of what has passed. But as I mentioned in earlier chapters, I press forward to the new memories and rhythms God is bringing to my life. Take time to grieve, Mama, and then take time to see new memories and new rhythms that catapult you into a different season— often a richer and deeper one, full of wisdom from the days past.

So what kind of parent are you? Does anything resonate with you from what I mentioned? Or maybe none of it did? Lol! That's okay too. Just find what works for you with your family and what you value but do take the time to explore what rhythms you want to have. Rhythms often flow with the season you are in, but the rhythm doesn't have to take over your life and peace. Ask yourself some questions:

1. Will I have certain family nights each week?
2. Do I want my kids to have some chores? If so, what does that look like and when will I have them do them?
3. Will I have parameters for screen time? (I had certain days of the week for "game time," and then during a school night, it was only an hour. Weekends were different, but nothing on Sundays.)
4. When my kids begin doing sports, will I allow them to do as many as they would like? Or will I limit the number of activities each season?

This is just an idea of questions you might ask yourself. Can you think of anything else right now as you are reading this? Why not take a minute and jot a few more down.

_____

_____

_____

_____

Awesome! Have I told you lately you are amazing? You really are! Yeah, you might say I don't really know you, but, my friend, you made it to Chapter 9. You decided to pick up this book with the interesting title to see if it might have a morsel to help you, and you realize it's better to do life with others. So let's rejoice in this because it is a victory to want to learn, grow, and fellowship.

And let's rejoice because it's time to leave the desert. You know, though, in the tough times, the dry times of life, when you feel like you are in a desert, God gives you an oasis if you stay the course. He gives you new dreams, new friends, and new places that feel like home. But there is a promised land the Lord is leading you toward, so embrace the lessons and new connections, but remember, there is always more for you! Where you are is not where you stay—at least not forever.

CHAPTER 9 QUESTIONS

What does Matthew 5:13 say about being a light? What does this mean? How can you be a light when you feel like you are in a desert?

What rhythms have you already established in your own life? What rhythms do you have for your family? Is there anything keeping your family from having healthy rhythms and communication?

If someone asked you who you are right now, what would you say to define yourself? Are you happy with your answer? What might you need to do to find a good balance in who you are and who you want to be? Maybe find one scripture that could be an anchor right now as you navigate YOU in this season. (I'll share mine at the very, very end of this chapter!)

(Move your eyes to the bottom of the page for the scripture I anchored onto many years ago.)

Psalm 37:4
"Delight yourself in the Lord, and He will give you the desires of your heart."

Chapter 10

Middle School Years

Setting New Goals for Myself before the Nest Is Empty and Doing Warfare over My Boys' Lives

For though we walk in the flesh, we are not waging war according to the flesh. For the weapons of our warfare are not of the flesh but have divine power to destroy strongholds. We destroy arguments and every lofty opinion raised against the knowledge of God, and take every thought captive to obey Christ . . .
—2 Corinthians 10:3–4

♪ DANCE PAUSE ♫
"Let Us Pray," Steven Curtis Chapman

C an you imagine wandering in a desert for forty years? I can't imagine that. The Israelites did this, and then many of them didn't even make it to the Promised Land. I was only in Alabama for four years, and I was able to eat more than just quail and manna. Thank goodness!! But seriously, I know there was a lot of praying in the desert and lots of time for soul-searching. A lot happened in Alabama to help stretch and grow me as well as prepare me for "coming home" to Ohio, my promised land.

At the river Jordan, the Israelites crossed over to their Promised Land (read about it in Joshua 3). All of us will walk through some lonely, desolate times in our lives at some point, but what can we do to be sure we don't have to stay there too long? Well, I can say one thing is to learn how to pray—I mean, really pray. It is one of the greatest weapons you have against the enemy, and it is the very thing that will get you through those tough times.

Some of the hardest times your kids will walk through are during their junior high or middle school years. I spent five years teaching seventh and eighth graders, so I became pretty familiar with all the things that can happen. But it's a little different when it's your own kids—in that you have a special authority over them that is very powerful. Let me tell you a little about that.

One of the Ten Commandments is "Honor your father and your mother," and in the New Testament in Ephesians 6:2–3, it also says, "Honor your father and mother (this is the first commandment with a promise), that it may go well with you and that you may live long in the land." It's pretty important for children to honor Mom and Dad in order to have a long, healthy life. Parents are also charged to "train up a child in the way he should go, and even when he is old, he won't depart from it" (Proverbs 22:6). We have a charge to guide our kids in their faith and help them to know Jesus, for they are a "gift and blessing from God" (Psalm 127:3–5). So, Mama, wondering who you are right now? You are your child's prayer warrior (and you will be all their lives!).

When you pray in the name of Jesus, you pray with God's power. In John 16:23, Jesus said, "Most assuredly, I say to you, whatever you ask the Father in My name He will give you" (NKJV). When you pray in Jesus' name, you are given authority over all the power of the enemy. Stormie Omartian reminds us in her book, *The Power of a Praying Parent*, that this "proves we have faith in God to do what His Word promises. God knows our thoughts and needs, but He responds to our prayers."[12] This is our weapon in the battle over our children's lives. We can pray Scripture over them and for them, and the Bible promises His Word will not return void, and it will accomplish what the Lord desires (Isaiah 55:11), and God's Word is "living and powerful, and sharper than any two-edged sword, piercing even to the division of soul and spirit . . . a discerner of the thoughts and intents of the heart" (Hebrews 4:12, NKJV). Isn't this just so stinkin' good?! Or, as my boys used to say, "Isn't this sick?" (Okay, that word has always confused me, but in this case, "sick" is a good thing. You're welcome!)

You are not powerless as a parent. No, you definitely are not! It might take some time, but praying the prayer of faith, it will come to pass! Time for a testimony! Buckle your seatbelts, Mama, I am about to share with you my oldest son's story. The enemy had a plan, but he didn't know my boy had a fired-up, praying mama!

But wait—can you just pause for a minute and write out Hebrews 4:12? This is just so good, and I really, really want to be sure you remember this verse. Ready, set, go! Write!

Hebrews 4:12

_____

_____

_____

_____

_____

(I gave you lots of space, especially for those big-letter writing mamas out there. I got you!)

---

[12] Stormie OMartian, *The Power of a Praying Parent* (Oregon: Harvest House Publishers, 2014), 18–19.

Nice, Mama, that was worth the pause. Hopefully, you didn't skip that part. If you did, just remember to write it down later.

So the story . . .

Hunter, as you remember, is my oldest son. When he was about twelve years old, he was frustrated and struggling with life. In fact, I came across a letter he wrote to me at this time while writing this book, and it basically said twice that "the world would be better off without me." ☹ Let that sink in. My precious boy was hearing a lie in his spirit. Where do those lies come from? Yeah, you got it, that jerk-devil I mentioned in the very first chapter. I took this moment in time very seriously, so much so that I kept that letter for twelve years. I prayed over it and rebuked the lies my son had heard, and then I took a step further, and I prayed over and with Hunter. I began a nightly ritual of talking to him about his day. We would rate it from one to ten, ten being the best. We would talk about the good and the bad and how all that made him feel. Sometimes, he struggled to tell me what happened or how someone wasn't nice to him, but gently, I guided him through the tears and the anger. It was powerful to see some of his burdens lifted from him. He began to make peace with himself and how God designed him to be. Writing this right now brings tears to my eyes. It was many years of doing this that made the difference. Navigating the middle school years is not easy for anyone, but it's much harder if your kids don't feel they have someone to share the hurts and hurdles they may be facing.

I am so thankful to say that today Hunter is a force to be reckoned with on the Kent State University campus. He shares his love for Jesus with college students with his wife, Nadia, by his side. The enemy wanted to take this son of mine and destroy him. He prowls around looking for who he can devour, but don't you think for a minute that he is more powerful than Jesus, who was raised from the dead. It's a battle, mamas, and one you enlisted in on the day you became a parent. Pick up your sword, the Word of God, and go to battle! You are promised the victory!

I prayed through the *Praying Parent* daily for my four boys for years and years. I recommend buying your own copy. It is full of scripture for how to speak over all situations your kids may walk through, from securing protection and resisting rebellion to having godly friends and being free from fear. I absolutely love this book because it points parents to the Word and how to say it aloud for every detail of your kids' lives. As you pray, you will see your kids move from their desert experiences to crossing the river Jordan to their promised land.

So good, right? Not only are you a prayer warrior, Mama, but you also are a daughter of God who has gifts, interests, and talents. During these middle school years raising my boys, I began to think about what I might want to learn more about or what I might like to do as my boys needed me less and less. My first plan was to learn all I could about natural health. I signed up to pursue an online degree to become a naturopathic doctor, but eventually, I settled for thirty hours in clinical health. I enjoyed learning all I could, but it just wasn't the thing I wanted to do for the rest of my life. So I prayed . . .

I began to realize I was really good at teaching English and knew this area very well . . . why not get my masters? I researched and decided to attend Liberty University online and get my master's in teaching and learning with an English cognate (fancy for English focus). I would pursue this once Hunter was a senior in high school, but for now, it was a goal I had to better and challenge myself and maybe someday get back into teaching. This is not for everyone, I know, so please think within who you are and how God has made and designed YOU. This is not a competition. All of us need to be as God made us to be, so stay in your lane, live out your unique story, and be the best YOU that you can be since there is only one of you. Because, Mama, God made you where you are for "such a time as this," and you may think He is done with you in this season, but He isn't done with you yet!!

As the middle school years marched on for all my boys, we had band concerts, track meets, basketball games, lacrosse, and lots of football games. Life was always busy, so taking time in the summer to be intentional helped create some of my favorite memories with my boys. We not only made many trips to Wildwater Kingdom water park in Aurora, Ohio, but we also continued our tradition of Monday night library visits that helped all of them meet the Chenevey family summer reading challenge. Ah, yes, the summer reading challenge in our house meant if you read a certain number of books by the cutoff date, you could be the lucky winner of the video game of your choice! This was the coveted prize for all middle school boys, and wow, did they read and read and read! Whatever it takes, right, Mama?? We also ended the challenge with a trip to Chuck E. Cheese. I'm not sure who had more fun, the boys or me. Ha ha ha! I always missed my boys when it was time for school to start because we spent the summer having fun together. Priceless memories are the ones that last a lifetime.

Maybe you are homeschooling your kids and just need to change up the routine when it's summer. What are some things you can do? Or maybe you like to go camping or work on projects together in the summer. Whatever it is, think of things your child or children like to do and find relaxing. Then, incorporate that into your summer memories. Even if you work during the day, find moments after work that help you connect in different ways during the months without the stress of school. You'll find some wonderful moments of laughter in the midst of it all, and someday, you will look back and be glad you took the time to be intentional.

PHEW! Soooooo heavy, you say? Is it time for a break? Think of one of your favorite songs . . . yes, think of it right now. Did you find one? What is it? Now, stand up and go and play that song. As it plays, I want you to dance, march, whatever it is you do when you get on your groove, and then imagine you are crossing the Jordan River like the Israelites did years ago. And imagine the joy of entering the Promised Land . . . your promised land that God has for you as well as for your children. Then, take a deep breath and thank the Lord for getting you to where you are now and for helping you discover some truths about YOU and what God still has for you in this season. Next, trust Him as he leads you into this promised land. Although it is unknown, too, like the desert, this time in this place, you will thrive and grow and jump for joy! So let's go, Mama—get your groove and dance into all that God has for you right now. You got this, and God's got you!!

CHAPTER 10 QUESTIONS

What does the Bible say about how children should treat their parents? What happens if they do?

What amazing truth can be found in Isaiah 55:11?

What would you need right now to feel that you are in your promised land? What is the main thing you can do when you or your kids are walking in a desert experience or challenge?

DANCE PAUSE
"I've Got a River of Life," Sunday School Singers

The song that came to me at the end of this chapter is "I've Got a River of Life." Take a moment and listen to this song and focus on the lyrics as they remind you that Jesus flows through you like a river, and, as you enter your promised land, He brings freedom, healing, and hope.

Chapter 11

High School Years—
Celebrations Galore

The Power of Conversations

For everything there is a season, and a time for every matter under heaven: a time to be born, and a time to die; a time to plant, and a time to pluck up what is planted; a time to kill, and a time to heal; a time to break down, and a time to build up; a time to weep, and a time to laugh; a time to cast away, and a time to gather stones together; a time to embrace, and a time to refrain from embracing.
—Ecclesiastes 3:1–5

♪ DANCE PAUSE 🎵
"Love Life," Jason Gray

Embrace—it's a word many of us know. If you close your eyes, maybe you envision two people hugging after not seeing each other for a long time, or maybe it's just two people who embrace in a moment of grief. The Oxford Dictionary says embrace not only means "holding someone closely in one's arms" but also means to "accept or support (a belief, theory, or change) willingly and enthusiastically." So embracing ALL seasons of your life, as well as your kids' seasons, helps you LOVE the life you are living even more. Sometimes, life is so busy that you can't see the end when all you want to do is collapse on the couch. But maybe if we take a moment to see the joy in the season we are navigating, albeit very busy, we can learn to "love life" and see it love us "right back."

What in the world does that mean? Jason Gray's song "Love Life" used to make me happy every time I heard it years ago, and hearing it again as I write this chapter does the same again. Another verse says, "If you're holding every moment just like it was your last, then you know that if you love life, it'll love you right back." I sense a deep gratefulness in all this. If we can get ourselves to a place where we can enjoy and embrace each season, we will have no regrets. We won't miss the here and now, wishing the present moment away because it's just too much or too busy. So here we are (well, at least here we are for this chapter!); it's high school years, and you find yourself allowing your son or daughter to get behind the wheel of a car. Let me tell you, if you haven't reached this season yet, there is a special "club" for all parents who have passed this training time. Not only does it take some special patience, but it also requires an abundant amount of fervent prayer.

I would usually pray Psalm 91 out loud and often speak parts of it over my boys as we would drive off together, but especially any moment they were driving on their own. We have the promise that if we say, "The Lord is my refuge" and make the Most High our dwelling, "no harm will overtake you" (verses 9–10). And my favorite part to pray over them are verses 11 and 12, "For he will command his angels concerning you to guard you in all your ways. On their hands they will bear you up, lest you strike your foot against a stone."

Remember, the Word is powerful and active, and especially when we speak it aloud, it "does not return void" (Isaiah 55:11). Take authority over your kids, and as you do, you teach them to do the same for themselves. This action helps them see they have strength and power in the Lord, and they also have the Word of God to use as a sword in all areas of their lives. This increases their faith and helps them have peace as they go about their every day, and so will you, Mama, as you exert the authority Jesus has given you.

(God Pause)

Break time!! Yes, time to think about a few morsels of truth that we just discussed.

What does it mean to embrace the season you are in? What does that mean to you? Can you explain how it makes you feel to embrace it all? In this embrace, what scripture can help you take authority and have peace in some of the times you need protection for your kids? Take a few minutes to jot down some things going through your thoughts right now. Then meet me below—about five "returns" of the keyboard.

Excellent! Now, let's get to it! I titled this chapter "Celebrations Galore" and the subtitle "The Power of Conversations." Interesting mix, right? High school is a time filled with lots of hurdles for your kids, but in this, there are many opportunities for celebration. Let's start there . . .

Having four sons means lots of activity. Hunter was a big football guy; Luke did lacrosse for a few years and then spent time volunteering and serving kids through Huddle/Shuddle and tutoring. Blake tutored, played trumpet, and excelled in track; Hayden played basketball, ran track, and played football for three years. It was a busy time for over a decade, with lots of banquets, ceremonies, and birthday parties. Being busy is fun, but in the busyness, it's important to have conversations in the midst of all the "stuff."

But in order to have good conversations, my hubby and I showed up. We coached, asked questions, cheered the loudest from the stands, and prayed through injuries and frustrations. Our boys knew we cared about their lives and what was happening because not only did we show up but we were also available when there were only ten minutes to talk between dinner and homework. I often stopped whatever I was doing and listened to them. After the years of driving with them in the car were over, these pockets of time to talk were treasures, and these treasured moments, I believe, became the bedrock of what kept our sons healthy and stable.

Knowing someone is always there to talk and listen, no matter what they are talking about, helps kids feel heard and seen. This is such an important need for teens, and I feel it is a big part of their identity development. And it's so good if our kids can feel they can talk to their parents rather than always going straight to their peers. Why is that so good? Well, I'll tell you, but I know you already know the answer, but let's get it all out in the open since we are talking about the power of conversation!

If your kids hear truth from you, it's better than hearing something that might not be truth from a well-meaning friend or acquaintance on social media. This is also why it's important to have your own quiet time, reading and saying the Word, as well as meditating on what God says about us. Since the mouth speaks what the heart is full of (Matthew 12:35), then we best be careful what we feed our spirits! So this is the place to start. As we are filled up, we can pour into our kids when they need it (which is pretty much every day!).

What did this look like in our home? Conversations happened in the coming and going—in the car (before driver's licenses), in the driveway, in the kitchen when they grabbed a snack, and in the hallway when just getting home. These were not planned, get-it-on-your-calendar events, but rather, these were SEE IT, STOP IN YOUR TRACKS, and DO IT! I had the luxury of not working full-time while raising my boys. I made sure any volunteer work at church or for the school was done before my boys came home, which was at varied times. Knowing their schedules each day was important as well. Be sure you know where they'll be, and then you can be around when they return. My neighbor used to laugh as he would see me razor scooter by his window (as he was working from home) to the bus stop for many years, and shortly after the razor scooter run, he would then see me walking my dogs. This was because I would meet my middle school son as he got off the bus, and then the next would be the elementary bus. This is where the seed to "talk" was planted and became a routine in their busier high school years (and boy, was I in good shape during the bus stop years)! Ha ha!

The conversation . . .

What did it look like? How did it start? Sometimes, it was just my simple, "Hi! Welcome home!" I would meet them at the door every time they returned and wanted them to know they were important—that their arrival was a happy thing! Sometimes, I would ask, "How was your day?" Well, probably every time. Not the best way to get a conversation going for the son who didn't like to talk or who was just hungry and tired, but it was a start. I would just be around and follow them to the kitchen. Then, food in meant possible conversation out! It was always a time of understanding them, seeing what bothered them that day or what filled them with joy. I would laugh with them as well as cry and often pray for them. And when they had had enough, the conversation naturally ended, and I went back to whatever I was doing. I would do this again and again, depending on when each one of them left or arrived home. Every morning was also spent with me sitting at the table, whether they talked or not, and then I always took time to pray over them before they left. Simple but beautiful little moments that added up over the years, not only in our relationship time but also in the words we had with each other. I deeply miss these moments as I am writing this today ... but grateful.

(*God Pause*—and for me, a moment to grab a tissue after reliving this memory.)

How are you feeding your spirit? What are some ways you can regularly challenge yourself to grow in the things of God? What is the verse that talks about how what's in your heart will come out in your words?

Conversation. Powerful. Necessary. Crucial. Life-giving.

Be real with your kids from day one, and it won't be hard to be real all the years of their lives. Taking time to teach yourself what works with teens and what doesn't is also helpful. Keep praying through the *Praying Parent* book I mentioned earlier too. It contains tools that can help you along the way. Take time to be intentional during this season of your kids' lives, and you won't regret the power of conversation in who they become and how they feel about who they are.

Another place to have conversation is around the dinner table. We always tried to do this as a family as often as we could. Even when my husband traveled a lot, we would include him through a Skype call, but always on the weekend. But even if it is just one parent, or if you are a single parent, take time to schedule dinners where you can sit down together. So much can happen over a meal. The pastors of the church I am attending presently always would ask certain questions of their girls around the table, which I love. These questions would cover the good in their day (things that made them happy or made them laugh), as well as the bad (what made them mad or sad), and lastly, a lie the enemy tried to get them to believe. This is a very intentional way to uncover some hard stuff that needs to be brought to light. The Bible says, "For there is nothing hidden that will not be disclosed, and nothing concealed that will not be known or brought out into the open" (Luke 8:17, NIV). Eventually things will come out, but in asking questions, we as mamas can help take authority over anything needing to be cast out or help our kids find healing in the everyday stuff before it becomes a lifetime issue.

There is power in conversation.

There is power in connecting with one another.

There is power in helping our kids know we see them and we care.

There is power in a family that takes time to listen and talk.

Conversation also can take on the power of prayer and the power of a testimony . . .

- Hunter began high school with friends who influenced him in negative ways. He displayed some negativity and rebellion that we answered with not-the-fun-kind-of-conversations, but the necessary ones where a phone was taken, etc. These were not fun, but we still intervened in conversations that helped him see our concerns. Testimony—By the time he was a senior in high school, he chose to be baptized and was voted "chaplain" of the football team!!

- Luke navigated a high school relationship that he knew needed to end, but the power of praying and talking him through the many months leading up to it would have been different without conversations. Testimony—God brought the BEST wife who was designed just for him, but in the pain and loss, Luke was better able to discern who was best for him.

- Blake missed his junior year of track due to COVID-19 in 2020. Many tears and conversations later, his senior year arrives, more conversations and praying, sowing seed, and speaking life over his season through an injury. Testimony—Blake went to states in THREE track events!

- Hayden did not make the basketball team in seventh grade, but through prayer and conversations, he believed in himself enough to try out again. Testimony—he made it in eighth grade!

In all these struggles, our boys found hope in what God could and would do in their lives. We, mamas, are just a conduit for helping our kids have healthy identities that are grounded in Christ. Without conversation, it's much more difficult to find hope in the darkness. Jesus gives us His Word and the power of conversation to help light the way for our kids. Let's rejoice in this truth and remember to "SEE IT, STOP IN YOUR TRACKS, AND DO IT." Seize the moment to have a conversation; don't let it pass you by. It will save your kids from the battle of an unhealthy identity.

CHAPTER 11 QUESTIONS

What does Isaiah 55:11 say? Why is this important in our walk with our kids (as well as our own lives)?

Why is conversation important in your kids' lives? What might a conversation look like with your kids in elementary school? Middle school? High school? Depending on where you are in your season of mommyhood, what are ways you can be intentional with your kids (Whether they are still at home or not)?

What does Luke 8:17 say? What can you learn from this scripture about the importance of having conversation with your kids in all seasons of their lives?

Chapter 12

Graduations, College Launching, and Funerals

Grieving Change and Leveraging a New "Normal"

*The Lord is my shepherd, I lack nothing. He makes me lie down
in green pastures, he leads me beside quiet waters, he refreshes
my soul. He guides me along the right paths for his name's sake.
Even though I walk through the darkest valley, I will fear no evil,
for you are with me; your rod and staff, they comfort me.*
—Psalm 23:1–4, NIV

♪ DANCE PAUSE 🎵
"Raise a Hallelujah," Bethel Music

Have you ever walked through a time when you thought you couldn't get your head above water? Sometimes, even when good things are happening, like graduations, you might find yourself happy and sad at the same time. Why is that? Well, I'm sure you know in your heart you are excited for your son or daughter who just accomplished an amazing feat, but on the other hand, that means the landscape of your life and home is about to change whether you are ready or not. Probably would be better if you were a teeny weeny bit ready, right? Sure, easier said than done, right? Don't put this book down at this point. Wherever you are in your mommyhood, this is good to read to prepare or to remember. Psalm 90:12 says, "Teach us to number our days, that we may gain a heart of wisdom" (NIV).

Number our days? Isn't that kind of dark and ominous? Well, it depends; in this scripture, we are to take time to be intentional, to reflect, and to be grateful for our moments and times with those we love. As we do, we gain wisdom that cannot be attained without experience, but that experience is also sprinkled with your diligence to reflect and learn—not just race through life till you stop breathing. No, that is not a healthy perspective. So what do we do with that here at this place in my story? Let's look at my first encounter with my oldest son's graduation and go from there.

In the summer of 2016, I decided I would begin my master's in English so I would have something to do when all my boys left the house. It was great in theory, but not in the actuality of having four boys living at home. Let me tell you, it was INTENSE! I was doing sixteen weeks squeezed down into eight weeks! As a result, in the fall of 2016, I decided to pause my endeavor and focus on being a full-time college counselor and advisor for Hunter. He began his senior year with my full attention, mostly because I had absolutely no idea how to navigate this season of life. How did I get to this point? Uh, Renee, it's called time marching on! Ha ha! Seriously, I had to get to grips with the reality of my sons growing up. Wasn't that the plan all along anyway? Teach them to be confident, independent young men so they can live out the purpose and plan God has for them. Well, yeah, but did it have to happen so fast?

Can you relate? If not now, you will one day. Maybe your son or daughter went to trade school and is about ready to go into the work world. Or maybe your son or daughter committed to serving in the armed forces. Any of these scenarios takes you to a moment where you realize, "Wait, he can't leave. I'm not ready yet!" That's what slowing down is for . . . give yourself some time to plan and think about what's coming. If you do, it will help immensely with not only the physical but also the emotional transition that comes with launching your precious child into the world. So here are some things I did . . .

I like notebooks. Yeah, I am a little weird that way. I like the three-ring notebook where you can put little dividers with labels. It's like my brain loves the order of this little thing. I can put all the flyers, the notes, and the research all in one place so my mind can rest a little easier than trying to always search all over the house for stuff. This is what I did for Hunter and all my boys. I had a "Senior Year Notebook." I began a comparison-of-colleges page with size, cost, pros/cons, and any notes if we visited. This was a lifesaver! And as Hunter narrowed his search, it was the perfect place to transition to his school-of-choice notebook. Ah, yes, I made another one! Now, I know I am from the "paper" generation, so whatever works for you, use it. Maybe it's an app, or maybe you are a Google Drive fanatic—use what works for you, but, by golly, Miss Molly, get organized (sorry, not sure where that came from, but I had to say it that way to keep your attention).

After this stage came preparation for graduation and a grad party. I don't want to spend too much time on that here, but you could always message me for any tips on what I did for graduation parties. A lot of that changed as COVID hit in 2020, but I had two under my belt by the time 2021 came along for Blake's graduation. I just had to do a little bit of shifting, but the plan was about the same.

(God stretch break)

Yeah, I'm sure He stretches too. Get up. Take a deep breath, and then breathe out. Ah . . . nice . . . great job!!!

So the plans are made, the party is ready, and the ceremony is about to begin. How do you feel? With each son, I had a mix of emotions of pride for their accomplishment but also one of bittersweet thoughts. "My boy is a man and only has a little longer in our home." Of course, I cried the day he graduated, but the hardest part came when we moved him out. (And at this point of my writing, I have moved three sons to college and two out and into marriages!) Again, it's wonderful and sad all at the same time. What's a mama to do? Cry and cry and just sit in that sad place forever? No! I'm sure you know that, but I can't assume anything. You do cry, but you also have to have conversations with your kids because they, too, are navigating some emotions and insecurities. The power of conversation is even more powerful in these transitional moments. Take the time to have them. You both will grow and feel better about what is to come.

Fast forward . . . Hunter is all moved in, and his room is empty at home. A year later, Luke graduated and moved to school too. His room was empty, and his regular spots in the house were empty. Give yourself time those first several days. It does get better, but it was tough. I missed them terribly, but I pressed into my Lord and Savior. I journaled, but sometimes I just listened to music and cried. I pressed into goals I had and into developing friendships. Again, I searched for things to challenge and help me to grow. All these things helped my soul and spirit transition and grieve and eventually embrace the new normal that was happening fast. I remember pressing into Isaiah 61:1–3 quite often, and little did I know how much after March of 2019.

Isaiah 61:1–3 (NIV) says:

> *The Spirit of the Sovereign LORD is on me, because the LORD has anointed me to proclaim good news to the poor. He has sent me to bind up the brokenhearted, to proclaim freedom for the captives and release from darkness for the prisoners, to proclaim the year of the LORD's favor and the day of vengeance of our God, to comfort all who mourn, and provide for those who grieve in Zion—to bestow on them a crown of beauty instead of ashes, the oil of joy instead of mourning, and a garment of praise instead of a spirit of despair. They will be called oaks of righteousness, a planting of the LORD for the display of his splendor.*

We will unpack this verse after I share something with you first.

Something happened in 2019 that rocked my world. I want to share what that was because if "she" were here today, she would also be someone I would want to mention as having an impact on my life and helping me in many ways as a bonus to my amazing mom I have mentioned before.

The Lord blessed me with a very special mother-in-love. Her name was Nancy Ruth Chenevey. My boys called her Gma Nani, and I eventually called her Mama C. She was in my life for twenty-four wonderful years, not nearly long enough, but I have a deep heart of gratitude for the time I did have with her. I was not only blessed to have a biological mom who loved me dearly but also was blessed with a kind, sweet, gracious mother-in-love. She poured her life not only into her own family but also into me, my husband (her son), and all her grandchildren. Things began to change in her health in January 2019. Little did we know that the cough she had back in November 2018 was related to what was going on in her lungs in January.

She went on her first dose of antibiotics with no improvement. She went on another kind since that one didn't do much, but the same thing—no improvement. By the time she was about to do round three, my sis-in-love and I both thought something was definitely wrong. I happened to get bronchitis on February 13, 2019. Two days later, after a dose of antibiotics, I felt like a new woman. I also knew then something was not right with Mama C.

On February 21, 2019, she was admitted to Alliance Community Hospital in Alliance, Ohio. We soon knew it was stage four lung cancer. She was not a smoker either; we wonder about many things that may have caused this, but I won't speculate that here.

We began our onslaught of praying and fasting and believing for her healing, but on March 13, 2019, Nancy Ruth Chenevey passed from this life to the next and into the arms of Jesus, only three weeks after her official diagnosis. We were all shocked, heartbroken, dazed, and numb. My life took another turn as I realized this special friendship was now going to have to wait till I passed into eternity.

Have you experienced a great loss? A sudden loss? What are ways you worked through your grief? If you'd like, jot those down right here . . .

_____

_____

_____

_____

_____

_____

Remember the verse I just mentioned above? Isaiah 61:1–3? One part of it says the Lord is giving us a "crown of beauty instead of ashes; oil of joy instead of mourning, and a garment of praise instead of a spirit of despair." When we walk through pain and suffering, the Lord promises to give us joy instead of mourning and praise instead of despair. How is that possible? Not at first do you just joyfully embrace your suffering, but as you grieve, praising and worshipping Him is healing for your body, soul, and spirit. Do me a favor; go to the beginning of this chapter and scan the QR code for the song "Raise a Hallelujah." Listen to the lyrics closely. Let the Holy Spirit wash over you as you listen. Then come back here. See you in a few minutes.

(God Pause)

So what did you discover? Our weapon is what? _____
What does that mean? As we sing, we chase the darkness away. We chase despair and hopelessness away. The enemy of your soul wants to grip you in sorrow and despair so that you will give up and not live out the purposes and plans God has for you.

Spending time with your Father in stillness or in worship is a time to renew and heal your spirit as well as your soul and body. He promises in Psalm 30:11 to "turn our mourning into dancing." Look that verse up right now and write its entirety below. It's so good, so I don't want you to miss this!

He clothes us with joy. He removes our "sackcloth of mourning." We are not to stay there. We have to get on with the business of living. Our life has a purpose. Our pain can make us better, but only if we let it. Our roots go deeper, and we become more empathetic and compassionate people. That's how Jesus wants us to be. He uses all our pain to make us better so we can gather more people to Him. Someday, "He will wipe away every tear from their eyes, and death shall be no more, neither shall there be mourning, nor crying, nor pain anymore, for the former things have passed away" (Revelation 21:4). Until then, keep fighting, sweet Mama.

Life keeps changing and marching on, but we are wise to take care of ourselves when we have so many changes. When we grieve our kids growing up and moving on, or we lose a close family member or loved one, we need to cultivate some rhythms to grow and be better than we were and more like our Savior. Here are a few things I do that I want to leave you with to end this chapter.

Renee's Rhythms of Life Suggestions

- *Community/Bible study*—Find good fellowship with other believers. Attend a good Bible-based, healthy, powerful church and get involved in the Word.

- *Prayer/quiet time*—Know the Word, pray in faith, speak life, stay centered, take communion, and most of all, take time to be still and LISTEN.

- *Worship/music*—Present yourself as a living sacrifice (Romans 12:1) as well as praise the Lord daily for the Lord inhabits the praises of his people (Psalm 22:3).

- *Journal/Writing*—See God's faithfulness and help work out confusion, pain, and disappointments. Record what God is telling you and have VISION.

These are, of course, suggestions, but some are necessary. You may already have some good and better things that work for you, and that's great, or maybe you can add something or improve what you already have going. Whatever you do, just be sure to take time to be intentional with your time and growth with God and other people. Luke 2:52 says, "Jesus grew in wisdom and stature, and in favor with God and man" (NIV). Jesus grew mentally, physically, spiritually, and socially—that's wisdom, stature, favor with God and man. So He's our example. Rest in this as you leverage new normals in every season. He understands. He sees you. He will see you through.

CHAPTER 12 QUESTIONS

What does Psalm 90:12 say? What does this verse mean to you?

What do we have to look forward to according to Revelation 21:4?

What are some healthy rhythms that you already have in your life to keep you tethered to the Lord? What are a few I mentioned that you can list here that you would like to implement?

Next chapter we'll see how life accelerated for me and my family. So buckle your seatbelts. It's going to be an exciting ride!

Chapter 13

Their Lives Begin— Career and Marriage

Learning to Grieve and Rejoice at the Same Time

Life is beautiful; life is beautiful
Living and dying, laughing and crying
If we have the whole world or have nothing
I know there are long nights, but we'll make it
With every sunrise comes a new light
Life is beautiful; life is beautiful
A father's love, a wedding dance, New Year's dreams
A toast with friends, a soldier coming home from war
The faith, the hope of so much more
A brand-new life, a mother's prayer
Shooting stars, ocean air, a lover's kiss, and hard goodbyes
Fireworks, Christmas lights
These are the things that make us feel alive
These are the times that make us realize
Life is beautiful; life is beautiful
"Life is Beautiful," music and lyrics by The Afters, 2013

♪ DANCE PAUSE ♫
'Life is Beautiful," The Afters

Change—it's inevitable, right? If I took a poll right now, many of you would say you are not a fan of change. Does that sound about right? We like the predictable and the comfortable, but by now, as a mama, you know that the unpredictable is pretty common. In fact, you have just about embraced the unpredictable, am I right? The moment you fall asleep after a very long day, then your sweet blessing comes in and is having a bad dream. Or maybe on Christmas Eve, after one son gets sick in his brother's bed, the other throws up all over the same son in the trundle bed. Been there. Done that. Oh, the joys of parenting. Or maybe when you change one diaper and then the toddler who is not yet potty-trained has a loaded diaper too. Or maybe it's the doctor saying your granddaughter needs help breathing for twenty-four hours, but everything will be fine. Will it? Ah, yes, the test and race of your faith.

Remember all the scripture you put in your heart years ago? Well, when the unpredictable occurs, that's when you reach deep down and see how rooted you are. You see if your foundation is true and strong. The storms come and rock your world. Maybe it's a good storm, like a happy time, but it is change. And any change seems to disrupt your peace a bit, right? You see your little boy all grown up as he awaits at the altar for his beautiful fiancé. You see your little boy hold his own little boy, and you wonder where the years have gone. But in all this, your heart rejoices in what the Lord has done. Your heart rejoices and embraces the new season coming. But I didn't rejoice at first. Let me tell you my story of change . . .

Imagine yourself graduating with your masters in 2019, just a month before your mother-in-love passes away, then you start a job after twenty-three years of being home, and then a worldwide pandemic breaks out only four months later in 2020 and shuts down life like never before. Next, imagine your house filling up again for six wonderful weeks with the children you raised, like a final farewell, all being together one last time. Then, your oldest son graduates online from college and starts a campus missionary job. Following this, your two oldest fall in love and get engaged within weeks of each other in 2021. Six months later, your third child goes to states in track and graduates from high school. A month later, your second oldest gets married, and three months later, your oldest child gets married. Phew! What a whirlwind! And that's not the end of it—Luke graduates from college in December 2021 and starts his career in January 2022. And in the same month, I experienced the sad passing of my dad on January 13. Many months are spent processing grief and managing his affairs. Five months after his death, beautiful Amelia was born on June 3, 2022—our first grandchild! Six months later, our first grandson, Caspian, entered the world the day after my fifty-third birthday!!

Four years of what makes life beautiful happens—four years of wonderful joys are sprinkled with some sadness and grief. For four years, life was navigating one day at a time, which was all one could do. One good thing is that all four years didn't happen at once. Those years were kind enough to unveil their beauty one year at a time, one major event at a time. And our dear heavenly Father only gives us what we can handle, or He provides a way out, so we are not overwhelmed with what we cannot bear, even under His protective hand.

First Corinthians 10:13 says: "No temptation has overtaken you except what is common to mankind. And God is faithful; he will not let you be tempted beyond what you can bear. But when you are tempted, he will also provide a way out so that you can endure" (NIV).

Amen! He always provides a way out (or a way through). He always promises to sustain us as we go through things. Even though I was rejoicing in all the wonderful, good changes my sons were experiencing, I also started to realize I needed to grieve what was no longer so I could embrace the new season I was entering.

Let me ask you. Is there a season of grieving you went through that you need to allow yourself time to be still in the sadness, the disappointment, or the change? If there is, take a moment now to take a deep breath, turn off any noise, and put your phone really far away from you. Just sit and be still for a minute or two. Ask the Lord to show you where you still need to heal, where you need to forgive, or where you are hurting and write that down here.

_____

_____

_____

Lay your hand on this book where you wrote that down. Now, let's pray this out loud:

Lord, I confess to you today this hurt, this disappointment, or this change I haven't fully healed from. I ask you to touch me right now. I ask for your Holy Spirit to help me release this pain and grief to you. I thank you that you are always with me, walking beside me. I trust you, Lord, and I know your plans for me are good. Forgive me for holding onto anything I shouldn't, and help me to move into the new season you are leading me into. I know I can trust you with my life in all ways, so I give you full control. Guide me and help me be led by you. In Jesus' name. Amen.

(*God Pause* Worship and Journal Break)

Ah, nice job, my friend! Now, I suggest taking a few more minutes to journal on your own or worship for a few minutes. I have always found both to be very healing. Write down any fears or thoughts you may be having, and then play a favorite worship song and sing loudly! Let your spirit soar as you praise the One who has you in the palm of His hand.

Welcome back! You are now ready to move into the embracing of the newness and change in your life. Whenever we go through change, we grow in our faith, but only if we yield to it and spend time in worship and prayer. Jesus is our example in how He stayed balanced and strong. Luke 2:52 says Jesus grew in wisdom and in stature and in favor with God and all people. I mentioned this in our last chapter. This scripture covers four areas we need to be tending to in our own lives. Being a busy mama makes this more challenging, but be gentle with yourself and do what you can. Jesus will do the rest, remember? Here are some questions I have for you:

- Mentally, do you challenge yourself to learn new things in every season?

- Physically, do you take care of the Lord's temple through good nutrition and exercise?

- Spiritually, do you make time with the Lord daily? Do you meditate on His Word when you can? Plug yourself into the Holy Spirit's power by renewing your mind daily.

- Socially, do you have fellowship with other believers and take time to be a light to unbelievers?

So how did I do these things, and how did I cope and grieve, you ask? Why, thank you for asking! Before I embraced it all, here are some things I did. I surveyed my life, and in 2020, I knew my job was too demanding for this season of my life. I had to move on to other assignments the Lord had for me. First step, I simplified. I also read a book by Gary Keesee called *Kingdom Thoughts: Your Roadmap to a Successful Tomorrow*. It's an easier read because it's basically like a devotional, although not with dates. It's packed with great, godly wisdom that really motivated me during this time. For example, one section is titled "Power-packed Prayer." Keesee says, "You're not going to be able to walk out His plan for your life if you're not listening to what He has to say. That's what prayer is."[13] He reminds us that "prayer is more than

---

[13] Gary Keesee, Kingdom Thoughts: Your Roadmap to a Successful Tomorrow (Faith Life Now, 2013), 21.

speaking. It's listening." During hard times, we can get caught up in just crying out to God when we really need to learn to listen. We just did this very same thing earlier in this chapter. See how I did that? We are doing things I have learned to do. But don't beat yourself up. Listening is a hard thing to do, and some days will be better than other days. Just do the best you can, and it will get easier.

Second, I immersed myself in the Word. I read, I sang, and I took notes whenever I could from church, from my own alone time, and with good, godly friends. And during this, I allowed myself moments to just cry as I missed having my sweet boys around. I cried over the season that was over for me, but I felt with each moment I allowed myself time to grieve I was healing. I was seeing through the sad clouds to where the rainbow of hope replaced the darkness (the rainbow is the original symbol of God's covenant with His people not to flood the earth again. It represents hope, so do not be confused by its misrepresentation in the world today. See Genesis 9:11–13).

Third, I kept the rhythms I mentioned in the last chapter, leaning heavily on socially engaging with others. I found myself intentionally planning regular lunches and dinners with friends or just a coffee break. Do whatever works for you, but find time to connect with other mamas and friends that are life-giving and encouraging. This is a time when you need others even more. Be sure to send that text, make a call, send an email; do what you need to do to make time for fellowship.

Finally, I tried new things. I taught online with a good friend who has a ministry in Ghana, West Africa, and I learned a new sport—pickleball!! My friend Kingsley asked me a few times to share with his community online. This was hard but well worth my time and effort to prepare to help encourage and teach those he was ministering to online. I also had a neighbor ask if I wanted to try pickleball. I was up for something new, so I said, "Sure!" I'll get more into that later, but in new seasons, when life changes, pray about what you might want to learn or try. It will be a way to heal and keep growing.

Second Corinthians 1:3–4 says, "The Father of mercies and God of all comfort, who comforts us in all our affliction, so that we may be able to comfort those who are in any affliction, with the comfort with which we ourselves are comforted by God."

What does this verse say to you?

_____

_____

_____

_____

_____

We go and grow through trials for many reasons, but one is to eventually comfort others in the same way we were comforted. How cool is that? We grow in our compassion and ability to love others better through our own difficulties. God gave us not only His Holy Spirit to comfort us, but He also gave us other believers. As I am writing this book, I realize and believe that my experiences have a purpose. I hope it is not only to encourage you but it is also to help you encourage those in your life.

Life is beautiful. Do you agree? The good, the hard, and the ugly—well, maybe not the ugly, but our heavenly Father promises nothing will be wasted (Romans 8:28). I have felt very, very deep grief and sadness, but I have also felt moments of wonderful laughter and joy. It is all about being human and living out the purposes for which God prepared in advance for us (Ephesians 2:10).

So, dear one, do not fear the changes, do not hold onto the past, but look forward to all the Lord has for you. Paul reminds us to "forget what's behind," look at what's ahead, and "press on toward the goal to win the prize for which God has called me heavenward in Christ Jesus" (Philippians 3:13–14, NIV).

This is what I tried to do, but sometimes God calls us back to the wilderness for a time. But do not fret and throw this book down and say, "Rubbish!" Rather, trust that I healed in my grief and was given a wonderful time to celebrate the abundant joys the Lord gave me, but after that, I deeply wondered, "What now?" I struggled for a while, but in the wilderness, I learned some of the greatest lessons of my life.

CHAPTER 13 QUESTIONS

What does the Lord promise in 1 Corinthians 10:13?

How are you navigating your life in the four areas mentioned in this chapter (mentally, physically, spiritually, and socially)?

I mentioned something about prayer that's important to remember, as highlighted by pastor and author Gary Keesee in his book *Kingdom Thoughts*. What was that? And why is this so important?

Chapter 14

The Wilderness

A Lonely Time of Wandering and Finding My Way out of the Wilderness

Been waiting on a moment, waiting on a sign
Waiting for them to call your name
And you're next in line
Waiting for your time to come, your fifteen minutes in the sun
Just let the ground rest cause if it's not right now,
It's for the best.
You're gonna grow; I know this.
But for now, just let the ground rest
Been waiting on a moment, waiting on a sign,
Waiting for the lights to change,
When you won't feel so stuck or so left behind.
Been waiting for the day to come
when you can leave behind what you've become
Wash it all away cause flowers only grow once they've tasted rain.
"Let the Ground Rest," music and lyrics by Chris Renzema, 2020

♪ DANCE PAUSE 🎵
"Let the Ground Rest," Chris Renzema

Wait! Weren't we already in the wilderness? I thought we already learned our lesson. Why, yes, but we may have several visits to this place in our lives, but every time we experience a wilderness, God is always there to provide the needed manna and guide us along. No one wants to stay in the loneliness and learning forever, am I right? So let's just get right to it. Why am I in another wilderness or desert? Did I make a choice that got me here, or did maybe God allow it to teach me some valuable lessons before my next assignment? So glad you asked! Sit back, grab a snack, and read on, my friend!

Interestingly enough, when the song "Let the Ground Rest" came out, it was the year of COVID-19, and the following year was my next visit to the wilderness. I know, so much fun in such a short time! Try very hard not to be jealous. Ha ha! But seriously, I know the outbreak of COVID was a very difficult time for so many, and really, for the entire world. I never want to minimize the intensity and uncertainty so many felt, as well as many lost loved ones during this time. This was a time when many felt their faith being tested in ways they never thought it would, but if you are on the other side, I'm sure you can see how God ministered to you even in this time of fear and uncertainty.

The same is true when you walk through these wilderness experiences in your life. God promises that He doesn't "give us a spirit of fear, but of power, of love, and of a sound mind" (2 Timothy 1:7, NKJV). The Word of God is our "manna" in these times of our lives (and all seasons, too), and it provides the necessary nourishment and direction as we navigate the "elements" of a wilderness experience. And this is exactly what He did for me.

In 2021, I just finished a year working for Malone University in their admissions office, overseeing all visits and events. It was a wonderful year of growing and stretching, but I knew God was calling me to let it go sooner than I expected. When I moved onto the next "thing," I found myself in the whirlwind of happy times of engagements, graduation, and two weddings. Being swept up in it all, I lost who and whose I was for a time as I tried to get my footing balanced again. Although I built my life on Jesus, the rock, I felt a bit overwhelmed by the many changes in my role as a mama. I was feeling no longer useful in some ways, maybe obsolete, as I looked on like a passenger waiting for the subway as one train passed by after another. I wondered where I was to get on next. What train would stop for me? I didn't know where I fit in anymore. I had a church community, but I was a new attender and felt lost there as well. It was certainly a Martha world, and I was feeling quite invisible. Have you ever felt that way? Have you ever felt like you were not being seen and no one really cared? Why not tell me about it in the space below . . .

_____

_____

_____

_____

_____

Feel free to spend more time here, but let me tell you, first and foremost, the enemy is a stinkin' liar!! The Lord says he SEES you. In fact, remember I said in earlier chapters He treasures every tear in a jar of alabaster? Psalm 56:8 says, God "keeps track of all my sorrows. You have collected all my tears in your bottle." Interestingly, the Greek word translated as "alabaster box" in KJV is also known as a flask, jar, or vial. The compelling connection here for me is that an alabaster jar is what the woman brought her oil in to anoint Jesus. This woman is Mary, Martha and Lazarus' sister. (Remember him? He died, and Jesus called him out of his tomb after four days! He was resurrected!) So tying this Old Testament gesture of God treasuring our tears is appropriate to the story mentioned in the New Testament when Mary cried tears on Jesus' feet and wiped Him with her hair; she then broke the alabaster jar that was filled with precious perfume/ointment (very expensive) and then anointed Jesus (read in John 12:3). This was a moment of love and reverence for Mary, as she showed her gratefulness to Jesus that is now forever remembered in all four Gospels.

So God doesn't just flippantly catch our tears in some Dixie cup; no, He collects them all in something that was treasured and represents something valuable. Therefore, we can determine that our Lord cares about all our trials and sufferings; He values us so much He collects and treasures our tears in a special, symbolic place. He shows His great love for us in this. Therefore, you can be sure, Mama, that He sees your life, even when you feel unseen. And He saw me even when I felt invisible. So let's get back to my little walk through the wilderness. I know, not a great hook to keep you here, but believe me, you want to hear what He taught me during this two-and-a-half-year journey.

I was busy in this wilderness time, but inside, I felt I needed to press into what God was teaching me as I felt unrecognized and pushed to the background in many areas of my life. As I write those words, it sounds like I had a problem with seeking approval, and I did. I now know that this was an unhealthy part of my personality that God said, "It's time to deal with this before I can use you in the next chapter I have for you."

I spent many, many years as a short-order cook, cleaning lady, playmate, psychologist, spiritual mentor, college counselor, nurse, physical therapist, taxi driver, event planner, school tutor, cheerleader, motivational coach, and writing editor. Sound familiar, mama of older kids? Sounds pretty good, right? But in all seriousness, these are very valuable "titles" and real-life things we do as mamas in our lifetime with our kids. It all started to feel as if every one of them was disappearing like a vapor, but I knew I was still needed deep within me. However, it was a struggle to accept my changing roles. I realized I needed to take some inventory of where I placed my worth.

Matthew 6:33 says, "Seek the Kingdom of God above all else, and live righteously, and he will give you everything you need" (NLT). What does this mean? First of all, as a believer, you will have a relationship with Jesus and a desire to get to know Him by reading the Bible, praying, praising, and fellowshipping with other Christians. All these things are great, but if you don't understand your identity in Christ, then all those "things" will do no good. I should have had this down pat, right? I mean, identity—it's the foundation of being a believer. But you wouldn't believe the number of people walking around who say they are Christians and don't understand this at all.

Identity. It is all wrapped up in what the Bible says about me. When I got saved, I became a co-heir with Christ (Romans 8:17). I inherited all that Jesus gave me, and this includes all the things He died and laid on the cross. I was redeemed from all sin, sickness, disease, poverty, and strife as it is under the Earth curse, and Jesus died as a curse for us (Galatians 3:13). Ephesians 2:19 says we "are no longer foreigners and strangers, but fellow citizens with God's people and also members of his household" (NIV). Pretty cool, right? We are members of His family, so we are His "kids." He chose us; we are His "prized possession," and He called us out of darkness into His wonderful light" (1 Peter 2:9, NIV).

Knowing who and whose I am helped me keep my eyes on getting out of the desert when the time was right. I had some good friends who stood by me and walked with me in my grieving and growing, and one such friend recommended a book titled *Anonymous* by Alicia Britt Chole. I voraciously read and cherished every page! I want to share some of the amazing treasures of this priceless and timely anointed work. But before I do, why not take a quiet moment in prayer? Think about where you are in the whole identity thing. Do you know who and whose you are? Are you struggling with this? If you are, think of a trusted friend or pastor you think you could talk to soon (and be sure you follow through). Feel free to use the space below. Then, see you back on the next page, in, well, as long as you need, my friend.

_____

_____

_____

_____

_____

_____

Anonymous, according to the Oxford Dictionary, means "not identified by name or unknown name; or having no outstanding, individual, or unusual features; unremarkable or impersonal." It's interesting to think Jesus really was unknown for thirty years, except for a little stint of teaching when He was twelve years old. He had "hidden years," just like we do. Another person in the Bible, Elijah, had three years of preparation before his big day on Mount Carmel (see 1 Kings 18). Before we talk about Jesus, let's see what we can learn from the Old Testament prophet Elijah. Buckle up, Mama, this is so good! I truly believe this is anointed for you to read at this moment in your life.

Elijah was this guy who came from a not-so-glamorous life. Based on where he grew up (Tishbe), we can ascertain he was not known. It's an area that's hard to pinpoint exactly where it is, but they can document Gilead, which is close to that area.[14] Gilead means "rocky" or "rugged," and it was a fairly remote and uncivilized area, so Elijah did not become who he was in a neat and tidy atmosphere or around the up-and-coming culture of a more urban, cultured city.[15] He was anonymous. He was unknown. He didn't have a hunger to impress. He was "perfect" for what God wanted in a prophet! But he wasn't just thrown into the biggest event of his life without any preparation. He was called to be bold on a basic level after years of seeking God, but then he was pulled back for three years to prepare for God's biggest showing on Mount Carmel. Where did God take Elijah for three years? What things were developed in him? What did he need to learn before he was released to be used by God in mighty ways?

Have you felt yourself standing on the sidelines of life? Where do you find yourself in the reading of this chapter? Are you wondering why you are seemingly in the background? Some of you reading this might like the background. Maybe you are being prepared in different ways to come out of hiding. What might God be developing in you that He wants you to use for an

---

[14] Priscilla Shirer, *Elijah: Faith and Fire* (Tennessee: Lifeway Press, 2021), 33.
[15] Shirer, *Elijah*, 34–35.

assignment "bigger than you"? Take a moment and reflect here about these questions. Then, meet me in the next paragraph to find out about Elijah.

_____

_____

_____

_____

_____

Elijah had to deliver a decree to King Ahab. It took a bold spirit that didn't care about being popular. God gave him what he needed to deliver this message. He says in 1 Kings 17 that there will be no rain till God speaks again. So I'm sure this was received very well, and everyone thanked Elijah. Ha ha! No—in fact, God knew there would be a search for him, so he instructed Elijah to get out of town to a place King Ahab didn't have jurisdiction, Cherith.

Not only did God call Elijah to physically relocate for his protection, but it was also a time to help Elijah grow in spiritual maturity. In these places God calls us, He does provide. He sent ravens to deliver food to him, and he drank from the brook in Cherith. He was seemingly hidden from society and Ahab's search party. He stayed here with all his needs met.

Even in our times of being in the background, God does promise to meet our needs, but most importantly, He helps us to grow and seek Him in these times when we aren't sure of our purpose or our next assignment. If we press into Him and His Word, we find rest for our souls, and we are nourished as we understand our relationship with the Lord in a deeper way when all the distractions are minimized. Jesus talks about getting away and resting in Mark 6:31: "Come with me by yourselves to a quiet place and get some rest" (NIV). And we also know that in these times of being pulled back from what's comfortable, the Word is "God-breathed and is useful for teaching, rebuking, correcting, and training in righteousness, so that the servant of God may be thoroughly equipped for every good work" (2 Timothy 3:16–17, NIV).

Elijah stayed and was obedient to stay till God said to leave. We often go to these places of solitude, feeling unsettled and restless. Is it time yet? Can I go, Lord?

We look forward to leaving rather than settling into what God wants us to learn while we are there. I know that for myself that I didn't like it at first. I was frustrated and sometimes jealous of other people's success or recognition. What about me, Lord? Haven't I been serving you well? Thank goodness that I felt led to press into my time with the Lord and what He was teaching me. It took some "kicking and screaming" at first, but when I did, He started to teach me about relying on Him, trusting in Him, hearing Him, and ultimately, knowing I can do nothing without Him. He is the one who gets all the glory.

I believe Elijah was about to do some really big things for God, and God had to get Elijah to a place where he would depend completely on Him and only Him before He could trust Elijah to do these great and mighty things for Him.

First Kings 17:7 says the brook dried up sometime later (possibly took years), and Elijah was called to do a few miracles. He first helped a widow in Zarephath who only had enough for a final meal, but the flour and oil never ran out as he stayed with her. Then, when her son became ill and stopped breathing, he performed a miracle as he laid on the boy and said, "Lord my God, let this boy's life return to him!" (1 Kings 17:21, NIV). I'm pretty sure this would give me some amazing confidence to do what Elijah had to do next . . .

Three years have now passed, and Elijah must go present himself to King Ahab again. Mind you, his wife, Jezebel, had been killing off all the Lord's prophets the whole time Elijah had been hidden. But he still made his appearance and was about to allow the Lord to use him to perform the miracle on Mount Carmel. He came to this point in his life bold, prepared, and ready for the seemingly impossible task about to happen. But impossible is not in the vocabulary of God. "But with God all things are possible" (Matthew 19:26, NIV). And, when we rely on Him and allow Him to work through us in our seasons of anonymity and our seasons of solitude, we are better prepared for the next assignment He has for us.

Elijah trusts God to provide, and at Mount Carmel, God shows up and makes fire on a drenched wood pile. He is shown mighty before the pagan God, Baal, and all his prophets. First Kings 18:16-45 gives all the details if you would like to read it. The main purpose of sharing this is how God prepared Elijah in his quiet and lonely season for the biggest moment of his prophet career. He was bold. He was ready, and he trusted God to show up because he spent time in the hidden season to get close to Him.

(God Pause)

What have you done to press in and learn when it seems God is far away? How do you steady yourself? What are practical ways you stay confidently tethered to Jesus during the confusing and trying times when you don't understand?

We can trust Him when we don't understand why we feel like we are unseen. You are being prepared, Mama! You are getting ready for your next step of obedience. Will you be ready? Will you take the time in your "hidden" seasons to prepare? That's exactly what I knew I needed to do, so I pressed in. One way I did this was by reading through the book I mentioned, *Anonymous*. Let's take a look together at what God taught me through this truly anointed writing.

Did you know Jesus was fairly anonymous for the first thirty years of his life? Nazareth is a place not mentioned in the Old Testament, whereas Jerusalem is mentioned over 650 times. Jesus was from a place no one really paid much attention to—perfect for a God-sized Savior of the world preparation. Out of the spotlight, hidden, and off the beaten path, that's where Jesus resided for the first three decades of His life. He was not celebrated because He seemed ordinary for the most part. Alicia Chole, author of *Anonymous*, sums it up like this: "So Jesus grew up as a relatively un-celebrated boy from an un-royal family in the un-respected town of an un-liked region. Bad news if you are running for office; good news if your job description is embracing hiddenness. Frustrating if you crave notoriety; freeing if you value learning without paparazzi."[16]

From the time we are born, we crave and desire—as well as *need*—attention. We want to be seen, and we need to be seen to survive as a baby and young child. As we mature, wanting to be the center of attention is one of those traits that can be, well, let's be honest, annoying to most everyone, right? We have to learn to be patient, to wait, and to have self-control when things don't go our way. But I still know our flesh desires to be good enough and seen all the days of our life; however, to truly be used by God, we have to crucify the flesh. And the best way to do that, in God's eyes, is to be taught and trained not to crave and desire attention from the world but, rather, to hunger and thirst for righteousness and intimacy with Him.

The life of Jesus really is an example of a life that was prepared, a life that was developed in the sacredness of being hidden. He embraced this time, like Elijah, and trusted His Father in the timing of being released to be used

---

[16] Alicia Britt Chole, Anonymous: Jesus' Hidden Years . . . And Yours (Thomas Nelson, 2001), 25.

by Him. "When he calls a soul simultaneously to greatness and obscurity, the fruit—if we wait for it—can change the world," Chole says.[17] You see, Mama, don't be frustrated by seasons of quiet and obscurity because this is exactly where God wants you to be. He is pruning you like a tree or bush so that you can produce more fruit.

John 15 specifically talks about how God will prune "branches" in your life not producing fruit as well as prune that which is producing fruit so it will "bear even more." Trust the "shears" of God, my friend. He knows what needs to be taken away and what needs training. I had to learn this, and I continue to learn it every day. But the key is surrendering to the process and leaning into the learning and growing.

(God Pause)

What do you think God is pruning in your life right now? What areas is He saying need to go? What parts of you and your life are being pruned to produce more?

(Note: Maybe this is something to commit to prayer for a few days. Pray and wait to see what the Holy Spirit says. Then, write it down and surrender it to Him.)

---

[17] Chole, Anonymous, 27.

I had to learn not to desire attention from people. I didn't realize how much I liked being in the spotlight till I was removed from it. I never was one to think I was better than others, but I liked cheerleading and being recognized for my achievements. I realized I liked the approval of the world, and if I wanted to go deeper, I had some pruning that needed to happen because, without it, I would find myself thinking I was "all that" when it was really all God in me doing the work.

You see, He must trust you with success. He won't use you till He knows you can handle the success where He gets all the glory. Now, I know sometimes when we rush ahead without His timing, we may still find success for a time, but many have fallen away when they thrust themselves into the spotlight before God said to go. You know why? It's because it's very, very easy to think, "Wow, I'm pretty awesome. Look at what I have done. Look at how great I am." In God's culture, this is not the soil where greatness is born. This is where self-centered, self-absorbed goals and plans are made.

That's not what God wants for you. If you truly are seeking Him and want to keep growing and being used by Him, you will grow in your maturity. How can you tell you are maturing? I believe it's when you know that you know that you know He gets all the glory, and you want Him to get it all!

When you are hidden, you can learn what motivates you and what you desire and crave because you are not getting those things. You'll see how you respond to others and their success and blessings. Are you happy and excited for others when good things happen? If you aren't, then buckle up—God has some pruning coming your way! But no shame here; we are all learning every day, and if we yield to Him, we learn what we need to mature in. So, if you press in during these times, you are being trained as you make decisions, as you give of yourself in different ways, and as you help and support others. The decisions you make in these wilderness years will give you an opportunity to learn how to make God-covered, God-yielded decisions in the future when He calls you out of hiddenness.

My time out of the spotlight began after I left my job at Malone in 2020. I entered an exciting season of celebrations, but I began to feel much of what

I knew changing and slipping away. It wasn't leaving completely, but it was changing, and I had to process how my role and roles would change as well. That was when I had days of wandering and days of chasing after job interviews and possibly teaching again.

But something in me knew this wasn't for me anymore. Doors closed left and right, and I felt rejected and sad, but God closed those doors for my own good. However, when doors close, we forget to trust that God didn't want us to go through them in the first place, right? But my flesh craved that attention, the "titles," the approval and acceptance. I struggled with letting go of all that and found myself wondering what was going on.

Reading *Anonymous* was truly life-changing as I began to embrace and understand doors closing, roles changing, and being seemingly unnoticed. It was painful and uncomfortable letting go, and then also painful to begin looking at myself more closely as I knew God wanted to use me again in the future. I had to allow God to prune me, to guide me, and to speak to me. He had to teach me to want His attention and acceptance above anything else. Another profound point Chole makes is when she says, "Our greatest enemy on earth is losing perspective and beginning to value our fragile surroundings more than God's faithful friendship in our lives."[18] My pursuit to achieve and be valued by the world had to change. I was good enough for a God who celebrated me whether I am known by the world or not; in fact, He rejoices over us with singing (Zephaniah 3:17). My relationship with Him had to be grounded and purified before I could ever walk in the spotlight again.

Therefore, as I write this book, I know its success lies in what God wants to do with it to touch and minister to people. I am just being obedient as He has asked me to use my gifts to glorify Him. And if God leads me into a writing and speaking ministry, I will feel myself tested in my spirit if it is successful. But my hidden years, if I allow them, will have created a foundation of humility that will keep my flesh and desires in check.

---

[18] Chole, *Anonymous*, 53.

Chole says one test during fruitful times is if "when receiving honor is no longer humbling, we need to take note. A great deal of difference exists between feeling honored and feeling worthy of honor."[19] This is so good. What is done in private will be even more important as success comes. As we navigate who we are as mamas in each season, we must never neglect our time alone in God's Word and submitting to His will, or we will allow worldly desires to captivate and distract us from God's best plan for our lives.

So as we leave this wilderness for our promised land, let's review a few key morsels of Truth:

- God celebrates us in all seasons of our lives. We are good enough just because we are His.

- When doors close, trust the Lord and know it is God protecting you. The best is still coming.

- Embrace times in the wilderness to cultivate what will be needed in the promised land. It is a time of preparation, so you are able to handle the success that comes as you leave a time of hiddenness.

- Pruning must happen so that even greater fruit can grow in your life. It will be painful, but it's necessary.

- Most importantly, humility is the key to staying grounded during the times when God is using you in your calling. It is what will guard you against seeking man's approval and attention.

Dear one, are you ready? The promised land is just around the corner. Come follow me as we explore what lies on the other side of our desert.

---

[19] Chole, *Anonymous*, 157.

CHAPTER 14 QUESTIONS

What does Matthew 6:33 say, and why is it so important as we walk out a time in the wilderness?

Who was Elijah? What happened to him? How did God prepare him for his big moment at Mount Carmel?

What verse did I mention about being pruned, and why is this process important?

What are two of the five morsels of truth I mentioned at the end of the chapter about what can be learned from the wilderness?

Chapter 15

The Promised Land

Blessings After the Nest Empties

He came to His own, and His own did not receive Him. But as many
as received Him, to them He gave the right to become children of
God, to those who believe in His name: who were born, not of blood,
nor of the will of the flesh, nor of the will of man, but of God.
—John 1:11–13, NKJV

♪ DANCE PAUSE ♫
"Just like Heaven," Brandon Lake

A child of God, our true identity—ah, that is the key. As you navigate
YOU through the seasons of life, the one thing that will keep you
forever grounded and tethered to God is knowing your identity.
And as we've reached the promised land in the happenings of my life, I am
believing that the Lord has also taken you through some things to refine and
define you according to what God says and not the world. But believe me,
I know it's a struggle. You will have to continually put on the full armor of
God daily and stay in the Word because, remember, you have an adversary
prowling around—and he would love more than anything that you never
reach your promised land.

So here we are. It's been a fun journey with you, but also one where I most definitely shed some tears. And I am guessing you shed some too. But what's the promised land like? It may look a little different for all of us, but I think we can all agree that there is fruit and abundance, but not perfection—we still may get tripped up here and there by rocks and gopher holes that get in our way, but we will be better equipped to navigate those distractions! So come along with me as I describe what I experienced in my own promised land.

The fruit of praying over my children consistently for many, many years yielded the crop of wonderful daughter-in-loves and grandchildren! Never stop praying for your kids and their spouses. You will see the victory if you don't lose heart.

As I settled into just resting in being a child of God, a freedom rose within me to start saying "yes" to some new things. One of the first things I said yes to was Young Life. I attended a Young Life banquet for the first time and found myself wanting to be a part of the organization that literally saved my life. Young Life is an amazing organization that sends volunteer leaders into public high schools, and now middle schools, to develop friendships with students with the hope of inviting them to Club. Club happens once a week in people's homes in the area; there's lots of crazy, clean fun—singing songs, playing games, and then a time to hear about who Jesus is and things He did in the Bible. As a freshman in high school, it resonated with my hurting and lost heart. I attended Club with friends from the basketball team, and then later I attended camp in the summer. This is where I gave my heart to Jesus, which, as I mentioned, saved my life and changed its trajectory forever. So, nearly forty years later, it was about time to give back!

I decided to help with the committee, which is a group of people who help support the staff and leaders. We all have different roles to fill, but each one is essential to the success of helping all those serving alongside so many hungry and hurting students. We have committee members serving in social media, banquet planning, prayer, fundraising, and leadership support. It's been a fun way to connect with new people and faces with the goal in mind to help spread the love of Jesus Christ. What a joy to know even though my life and seasons have changed, God still opens doors to use me in His plans.

Saying yes to Young Life also opened the door for me to speak publicly and share my testimony at our annual banquet as well as with a Fellowship of Christian Athletes group at a local women's prison. Being able to share my story and how I got to where I am was a powerful opportunity not only for myself but also for all those attending. They were able to hear how Young Life and investing in it can affect not only that student but also the future spouse and children of that student. And as a result of speaking at the banquet, I was asked to come share at a local prison. What a joy to bring hope to a place where hope may be somewhat lost in the darkness of being removed from the outside world. These women taught me about second chances and the simplicity of being a part of something bigger than myself. Your yes to things will not only bless others but it will also bless you!

(God Pause)

What have you said "yes" to lately that you can see is not only blessing you but others as well?

Well done, my dear friend! (It's okay I call you that at this point, right?) As you settle into who and whose you are, you can say "yes" to new things in new seasons of your life. This was just the beginning of figuring out what God was doing in and through me as I could see the life I knew as a busy mama of four boys was fading. In looking ahead, I was beginning to see an even more beautiful, richer, and fuller life on the canvas ahead. I started to get excited for the new ahead and not stay stuck in grieving what once was.

As a result of this, I knew I needed to challenge myself in other ways— ways where I found joy in competition or achievement. It was a part of me, having been an athlete all my life. The first challenge was to get my motorcycle license. I was always scared of this venture, but my husband encouraged me that it was something we could do together. I decided it was time to face my fear, and seeing a cool, green Benelli motorcycle helped the process as well.

Jeff, my son Hayden, and I stopped by a motorcycle dealership one Saturday afternoon. The moment we walked in, I was enamored by this flashy, little green motorcycle. Yeah, never thought I would say "enamored" about a motorcycle, but, hey, a new season, right? It was small enough that I felt I could control it, and the rest is history. We ended up purchasing that cute little thing—again, my husband would NOT say cute, ever, but he didn't care. I was aligning with one of his passions and that was all that mattered.

So the motorcycle before the license—kind of like the cart before the horse, but then, I was really committed now to the process. I began to read the motorcycle manual for the test. It was really hard! I actually did not pass the written part the first time. I was horrified. Ha! Well, it was frustrating, but I pressed in and read some more. The second time was completely unlike the first test. I aced it in ten minutes flat! I did what I needed in my mind, but now I had to apply it to the real thing. Isn't that a bit like reading the Word of God? Sometimes, we get all the head knowledge, but it's the application of it all that really matters. But in saying that, there has to be intentionality and preparation, and we must press in and know the Word, but then we have to have the courage to live it out. So that's what I did! I signed up for an Ohio motorcycle course.

This course required class hours as well as an entire weekend of being on a motorcycle in full gear, running through skills and training. This was not for the faint at heart, I'll tell you. But can I just say, don't decide to take the class in the heat and humidity of Ohio's August weather?! It was probably one of the hardest things I have done. But I pressed in and would not quit. I finished the course and passed the test! What a sweet victory! And, yes, it's time to reflect on YOU and something you need to face and what you can do to prepare.

What is something you want to do but you are afraid to try? Why are you afraid? How can you prepare to overcome this? As a believer, we face a battle every day. How can we be prepared as we walk out our everyday lives? How can we apply what we know?

_____

_____

_____

_____

_____

I still review the basic principles of riding, especially the safety precautions that must be taken to be safe on a motorcycle before I ever get on and ride around. And the same is true whether you have been a Christian for a year or fifty years. We have armor we need to wear every day (Ephesians 6), and we need time feeding our spirit on a regular basis so we can be prepared.

My next "new" thing in this promised land I was enjoying was the game of pickleball! My neighbor Kathy came to me one day and asked if I would like to play. I had no idea what it was, but it sounded fun, so why not?? And so it began—I also got to know Faye and Becky, as we four braved the cold to teach and learn from each other, setting up Becky's portable net. It was a really fun distraction for me as the house was now empty of three of my four boys. I also found joy in our newfound friendships with one another; we would laugh and talk and share our lives on the days we played. It was truly a gift God gave to me during a lonely time of transition. I consider these ladies very dear to my heart, as they encouraged me not only in playing but also in my new role about to burst forth as Grammy!

As I reflect at this point, one of my favorite verses comes to mind about not dwelling on the past and how God wants to do a new thing in and through you!

Isaiah 43:18–19 says:

> *Forget the former things; do not dwell on the past. See, I am doing a new thing! Do you not perceive it? I am making a way in the wilderness and streams in the wasteland.*

A way in the wilderness? Ah, yes! Remember the wilderness? Remember those times in your life when it felt dry and barren? Well, remember you are not meant to stay there! God kept bringing people into my life to remind me that change was necessary, but it doesn't mean your life is over just because something ends or your kids move on to live their lives. It just means it's time to see where God is making streams in the desert for you to follow. And, yes, even something fun like pickleball can be that very stream! It has brought me so much joy and laughter it's hard to explain. It's been a challenge to learn something new and exciting for my brain. I found a new passion, and I am grateful for my friendly neighbor who asked me, and I am glad I was willing to say yes. So be on the lookout for those moments when the Lord sends a nudge your way. You just never know what it will lead to and what it will do for your life.

I continue to play and improve today. I also have some new aches and pains, but I am learning to take better care in warming up, stretching, and not overdoing it. Of course, there's a whole other lesson there, right? It's important to try new things, but don't let it control you or allow yourself to obsess over it. Keep your priorities straight, and the new things can add that needed spice to your life when maybe it was feeling "flavorless." There is joy in the journey, and the Lord wants us to enjoy our lives. It's going to have its challenges, but it also is abundant when we allow it!

Can you think of a time when God created "streams in the desert" for you? Why not remember His faithfulness by writing it here? As we remember the times God has been faithful, it reminds us of His character and that He will do it again in times when we need a reminder.

Sometimes, we choose what we'll say "yes" to, and sometimes it chooses us! What I mean by this is, well, becoming a Grammy was something I didn't see coming so fast. But what a joy to experience this new season in my life. When Amelia Grace was born on June 3, 2022, it was an amazing and exciting time to see my own "baby" having a child. This was a joy I had prayed for over my children as they were growing up—that they would find a strong, Christian wife and have a healthy family. The Lord answered my prayer and then some because six months later, Caspian Joseph was born on December 14, 2022, just one day after my fifty-fourth birthday! I'll tell you, watching your children be parents is such a wonderful thing! I watch my sons, Luke and Hunter, delight in their kids, and I stop and thank the Lord for all the times I prayed for my boys and their lives. It was the best use of my time during those early years. What does God say about prayer?

Let's take a look . . .

Do not be anxious about anything, but in every situation, by prayer and petition, with thanksgiving, present your requests to God (Philippians 4:6).

> *Therefore, I tell you, whatever you ask in prayer, believe that*
> *you have received it, and it will be yours (Mark 11:24).*

> *Devote yourselves to prayer, being watchful and thankful (Colossians 4:2).*

> *Rejoice always, pray continually, give thanks in all circumstances; for this*
> *is God's will for you in Christ Jesus (1 Thessalonians 5:16–18, NIV).*

There's so much more, but I had to learn the process and trust God's hand and ear to hear. I was obedient and wanted to communicate with God, but I have to say, I wanted results, so I did it. But now, I realize it's so much more than that. I am reminded of Brandon Lake's latest song (as of the writing of this in 2024) that touched me and led me to a deeper intimacy in prayer and love for Jesus. Go ahead, get your AirPods or headphones on, and then find Brandon Lake's song, "Nothing New," from his *Coat of Many Colors* album from 2023.

♪ DANCE PAUSE ♫
"Nothing New," Brandon Lake

Beautiful. It's that simple. He just wants us to love Him, and He loved you so much He died for you. That, in itself, is amazing.

So, you see, Mama, this relationship with Jesus is the true foundation for how I navigated myself through these seasons of mommyhood. He was the one constant that never changed, and as I entered this new season of being a Grammy and getting ready for my last son to graduate from high school, I felt a call to challenge myself as this verse, found in some form in all four Gospels, began to resonate in my spirit:

> *All authority in heaven and on earth has been given to me. Go*
> *therefore and make disciples of all nations, baptizing them in the*
> *name of the Father and of the Son and of the Holy Spirit, teaching*

> *them to observe all that I have commanded you. And behold, I am*
> *with you always, to the end of the age (Matthew 28:18–20).*

The Great Commission is a call to go into all the world or wherever you live and be a light to others. I remember the moment I was sitting at the table with my youngest two sons and my husband on New Year's Day, 2023. We were thinking about a word for the year we felt the Lord was giving us, as well as a verse and some goals. I said I wanted to go on my first mission trip. And interestingly enough, God was like, "Okay, you got it! I have just the thing for you!" On January 8, 2023, a mission trip to El Salvador was announced for anyone interested. Right away, I thought, "Wow, that was fast." Ha ha! So after some prayer and conversations at home, my youngest son, Hayden, and I felt we needed to go. So began many months of trusting the Lord to provide financially and planning with our team. He showed up over and over through the generosity of a great number of people, and I felt my faith being stretched as the months turned into days.

Again, I kept having goals in these seasons of change and gave them to the Lord. This was something that really awakened me spiritually and pushed me beyond anything I had ever done. Two weeks before the trip, I felt a fear gripping me. It was really intense, but I prayed and trusted He would go before me and protect not only me but our whole team. And He did.

We left on June 1 and returned on June 10. We arrived at King's Castle in El Salvador and hit the ground running, practicing all the dances and skits for the kids' programs we would be doing. King's Castle began thirty-five years ago as a ministry dedicated to sharing the gospel with all the children of El Salvador every year. Teams fly in and are assigned leaders for the week. I had many divine appointments there, and you know, almost all of them were with women I came into agreement in prayer.

One encounter was with a twelve-year-old girl who had lost both her parents. She had run off from the main group, and I felt a nudge to run after her. Even with a language barrier, I just prayed and prayed. I felt her pain and just kept praying. I found the pastor who came with us and could speak Spanish. He agreed with me and informed me what she was saying. It was a powerful moment I would have missed if I had not been willing to hear the call, be stretched, and overcome my fears. The same can happen for you. Behind your yes is a life waiting to be touched by what you have to give!

By the way, I just so happened to be the oldest person on the team—so remember, age does not matter! If you are still here, God's not done with you yet! Yep, I said it. If you're a mama and over eighty, you still have something left to do. Just keep your eyes and ears open. And the same goes for the mama who is buried in loads and loads of laundry. When you are weak, He is strong, right? So keep your spirit in tune to people in line at the grocery store . . . or that mama struggling at story time. You don't have to jump on a plane and go to El Salvador to be on a mission. We are on a mission every day when we walk out the door or even stay home—social media can be used as a ministry!

(God Pause)

Take a moment . . . put on some instrumental worship music, get a pen and paper, and find a cozy spot. Take a deep breath and just be still for a few minutes. Ask the Holy Spirit what He would have you do that's new in your life. What does He want to challenge you with? In what ways can you be open and aware more of opportunities all around you? Set a timer for about fifteen to twenty minutes, and just write what comes to you. Maybe you'll even get a picture or a song in your mind. Don't overthink it. Just be free and go!! See you back here in about twenty minutes!

How'd it go? Maybe you can share it on my Facebook page (https://www.facebook.com/ReneeCheneveyAuthor). This is something I have been starting to do as a result of a mentorship program I am doing. Ah, you know what's next, right? Yep, I'm going to tell you about it.

But before we get into the amazing steps of how God led me to it, let's start at what I said "yes" to that led to my saying "yes" to mentorship. I received a Facebook Messenger invite from my friend Amy. I knew her from a Bible study she led seven years before, but the Lord had our paths cross once again when she invited me to a prayer HUB she was leading. I prayed about it and felt it was what I had been looking for the last several years. I showed up, and right away, I knew something was fire about this group. I would be back for more.

As the months passed by, I stayed committed and wanted to grow and grow. Amy kept talking with others there about some mentoring thing they did. Finally, after eight months of this, I said, "I want to do it!" Amy invited me to a retreat weekend with this ministry. It was an amazing time of worship, teaching, and fellowship, and they also talked about growing through their mentorship program. So I prayed and then signed up for the program. At this point, it was just to get information, but once again, I was excited to walk through an open door that not only excited me but would prepare me for the new season of life and what God had for me to do.

It was exciting to realize that the Lord, once again, wasn't done with me! I spent the next few months praying and still serving. One of the pastors at our church asked me about another mission trip to New York. I kindly declined: "That isn't for me." A month passed, and I was casually asked again. This time, I wondered if I was to pay attention. I felt deep in my heart that the Lord was trying desperately to get my attention. But it was right before Christmas, and I would get back on my birthday. I was thinking about the nice, tidy package of being called to do something, but God was saying it's not always going to be convenient or perfect timing when He wants to use me. I took it to prayer and felt peace almost immediately.

I have to say the trip was amazing. It stretched me and created a new surrender in my heart to the things God was showing me and the people He wanted me to touch for Him. I learned how to yield better and be aware, and that, my friend, has taken me to a new level of service to Him in a NEW season. I plan to write in more detail about these various encounters in another book, so stay tuned!

After New York and into January, I began my mentorship journey. I knew in my spirit that this was something I needed to do before the Lord could use me in this ministry of writing and speaking. I had to go deep, through layers of life, and find healing for those hidden places that only had a surface "cleaning" and were patched up without a full cleansing.

(LET'S THINK ABOUT THIS MORE!!)

So let me ask you something, are there places in your heart that you know you avoid thinking about? Or think about how you respond in situations where you just don't understand why you responded a certain way. For example, as I was pulled back from "getting attention" and being in a position with a title or authority, I found myself insecure, maybe a little jealous of others, and often sad about my life. I quickly realized that my identity still wasn't settled. I still needed to do more "work" on knowing WHO and WHOSE I was. I had the Holy Spirit in me to guide and counsel me, but I also needed to nurture and grow in the fruit of the Spirit in my life.

And one way to do that is through having other strong, powerful Christian women mentor you. That's exactly what Jesus did for me through this mentorship program. But before I go into what God has done and is doing through that, let's explore YOU.

Where are there places in your heart that you avoid thinking or talking about? What events, people, or places trigger unhealthy responses from you (i.e., anger, sadness, offense, rejection, etc.)? This is not to just leave you hanging but to help you see some things and get them out in the light because that's where things are exposed and then can heal. The enemy of our souls wants to keep things in the dark so that we don't move ahead in victory. But, Mama, Jesus came so you could have LIFE (and victory) and life in abundance (John 10:10)! Take at least ten minutes, play some peaceful worship music, and ask the Lord to show you what still needs healing in your heart. He'll show you. Take as long as you need. See you back here when you are ready.

_____

_____

_____

_____

_____

_____

_____

_____

As I write this, I am praying for you, my friend. This is hard stuff. You might not like how it feels, but don't throw this book down in frustration. Remember, you reading these words right now is not by chance. Jesus has a plan to heal you, and that brings freedom. In freedom, you can serve Him better because you are healthier! No matter where you are on this journey of mamahood, young or older, there are still people to help and serve in your sphere of influence, and you do that best when you are healthy! Let's take a deep breath right now—breathe in . . . breathe out. Again. Ah, that's good. Ready to move on? You are not alone—ever. Before we move on, let's say a prayer for what God is doing.

Thank you, Lord, for all that you are revealing to my friend reading this right now. Thank you for your hand upon her. Cover her right now with a blanket of your love, peace, and protection. No plans of the enemy will prevail to rob, steal, or destroy this peace or the plans you have for her, in Jesus' name. I agree right now with her that healing will continue, that she will find freedom in this and that you go before her and will never leave her or forsake her. In Jesus' name. Amen.

So the promised land is one flowing with milk, honey, and—freedom! For my own journey, I see the wilderness not always as just a place of bondage but as a place of searching, pruning, and learning, which leads to freedom and joy in the promised land. In some ways, it has been a long journey of finding healing from the sins that found their way to me, but it's part of my story and who I am today. Plus, it gave me a lot of good material for writing!

Here I am today. I am doing work, still, while in the promised land. Even in the "good" seasons, we still have work to do. We still have ways we can be better and focus on pruning the fruit in our lives. Galatians 5:22 says, "But the fruit of the Spirit is love, joy, peace, patience, kindness, goodness, faithfulness, gentleness, and self-control." It's always good to take inventory because we are a fragrance in how we treat people and exhibit this fruit. We want to be a "pleasing aroma of Christ" to not only God but all those around us (2 Corinthians 2:15).

One way God pruned and helped me grow was through a mentorship program I mentioned a few pages back. It was a time of getting in the Word, understanding again who I was as a child of God, and being refined by others doing the same. It was true "iron sharpening iron" (Proverbs 27:17). As you seek the Lord for growth, you'll find it, as I did. Through this, I began to grow in my faith and heal from hurts in multiple ways and through multiple layers. Part of getting to the promised land is dealing with the hidden places in your heart and spirit that want to stay hidden. When you allow the light of Jesus to shine in these places, He promises to turn your darkness into light (Psalm 18:28).

Here we are at the end of MY story. Thank you for taking this journey with me and seeing it through till the end. One more chapter to go that highlights the thoughts and insights from various mamas of all ages. I wanted to celebrate the many mamas I have known in my own life and give you a glimpse of their journeys, new or seasoned; we can all learn from one another. As we close Chapter 15, let's take a minute to review with a few questions.

CHAPTER 15 QUESTIONS

Write Isaiah 43:19 below. Then, take a minute to reflect on ways you know or believe God is making a way for new things in your life.

Find one verse I mentioned about prayer and jot it down here. Why did you choose this one? Take a minute to write out what's on your heart.

What is the Great Commission? Where can you find it in the Bible?

See you in Chapter 16, my friend!

Chapter 16

Words and Wisdom from Moms of All Ages

Welcome to the final chapter of *Hey, Mom, God's Not Done with You Yet*! And you will see, no matter what age you are, God always has a plan for you still being here—so He is most definitely not done with YOU yet.

I was able to survey thirty-eight moms from all walks of life, ages, and personalities. I asked them four main questions. All their answers won't be listed in their entirety here, but here are the questions I asked to give you an idea of the focus for the next several pages:

1. What is your favorite thing about being a mom?
2. What is the hardest thing about being a mom?
3. Do you have a favorite Bible verse or quote, and why is it special or meaningful to you?
4. What is the best advice or something you learned at this point in your mama journey you would like to share?
5. Anything else on your heart you would like to share?

I believe I would like to honor the two moms who have been at this for the longest as the first entry of this final chapter—my own mom, Dee, eighty-one, and my mother-in-love's only sister, Connie, eighty-four. I think you'll enjoy the simplicity of their wisdom.

Dee Frantz, My Mama!!

My mom has always taught me so much about laughter, so I enjoyed her favorite thing about being a mom: "love and laughter." I would have to agree laughing with my four boys is just the best. Loving them was easy, even in the hard, trying, lack of sleep times. On the other hand, the hardest thing is pretty much the same across the board for all the moms who have older kids, and that's "witnessing any pain, disappointments, and hardships." It's so hard to see our kids hurting and in pain, but isn't that how our heavenly Father operates as well? This puts it in perspective, right? He is saddened when we are hurting or struggling—in fact, His love for us is exactly why He sent His only Son to die for us!

For all my years being alive, my mom has always quoted her favorite scripture to us, and I know this comes from a deep heart of gratitude. "My cup runneth over" (Psalm 23:5, KJV). She always recognized blessings and would say this as she embraced her own kids, her grandkids, and her great-grandchildren. Good to remember to continually operate your life from a place of thankfulness.

Lastly, she provides the following advice: "Hold ALL your children gently in the palm of your hand as you LISTEN." Mmmm . . . so good, right? Hold your children gently because you have to allow them to go and grow, but listening is always a gift a mama can give her children of any age. She also says simply to "enjoy and love *every* minute." Live in the season you are in. Don't look too far ahead or wish the season away you are in. Embrace and enjoy it all.

And I would say she has. She showed up for EVERYTHING and gave generously of her time, her listening ear, her love, and her laughter. I appreciate who my mama has become, how she reinvented herself through hardships and heartache, and how she is finishing her race well—still loving her family, serving at church, and caring for other people. Thank you, Mom, for staying the course and not giving up. As this final chapter is being written, thank you for cheering me on and reading every word. You have done well. You are loved. You are appreciated.

Connie Post, My Late Mother-in-love's Sister

Connie, eighty-four, has five daughters and six grandchildren. She has had an abundant life of raising children and being a wife. One thing she says about one of the hardest things about being a mama is "giving yourself grace when you feel you've failed or made a mistake and remembering you are Mom, not God." It's hard to admit when we are wrong, but we are modeling humility for our kids and then grace and forgiveness. This is so good! We are not God. We will not be perfect, but we can know that through our mistakes, we can move forward and learn with our kids, as they are learning right with us! Such good wisdom!

Our impact as mamas goes way beyond the here and now. Connie adds, "Motherhood is a divine and unique calling that will make an impact on the next generation and generations to come." Imagine this for a minute—generations to come! What you do now will make an impact on your children's children and their children. Let's choose to make that a godly legacy!

And as our children grow up and move away, we can trust our heavenly Father to guide and protect them. Connie reminds us, "God continues to parent our children long after they've left home, and in that we can have peace." We train and coach our kids, but ultimately, they will have their own access to Jesus. They will have learned from you (and life's trials) how to press in and "seek first the kingdom of God" (Matthew 6:33).

Thanks, Connie, for your timely wisdom at different seasons of my life. You have taken the time to love not only me and your nephew Jeff but all my boys—especially as your sister was called to her heavenly home. You are dear to me. I appreciate and love you! Thank you for your perfectly timed texts and encouraging words!

***

Here we go . . . the final pages of my friends and family of all ages. These are their words, their hearts, their wisdom as they have lived out mommyhood. No matter how short or long that is, we can all learn from one another. Enjoy their responses!

QUESTION 1–What is your favorite thing about being a mom?

"Watching them grow in their love for Jesus and as their own little person."

~Kristen, 29, mother of two

"Watching my adult children have their own reckonings with God. Watching them question what they've learned and diving into Scripture on their own."

~Sue, 53, mother of three

"I loved every stage of motherhood, from the infant stages to the teenage years. I loved that the Lord gifted me with these precious beings and entrusted my husband and I to raise them."

~Gina, 57, mother of two

"Spending quality time getting to know my kids as young adults."

~Jen, 51, mother of two

"The unique relationship—it's unlike any other relationships in my life. Truly loving someone more than myself."

~Sue, 45, mother of three

"The unconditional love I receive from my sons and being able to spoil and nurture them."

~Cathy, 58, mother of two

"They are so brutally honest. And oh so fun. I can't pick one thing. They are fun. Just so so fun."

~Alyssa, 38, mother of two

"It's hard to pick just one thing. I love hearing him call me Mom, I love the way my heart leaps when he walks into the room, and I love watching him grow into a wonderful, independent man. I love late-night talks, hugs, and laughing till it hurts. I love our inside jokes and memories; I guess what I love best is the unconditional love and bond we have."

~Jennifer, 44, mother of one

"I think maybe the love that fills my heart for them. With all of our schedules being so busy, we don't see each other as often as I'd like. That brings a longing in my heart for them that I don't really have as strongly as I have for them and my grandkids."

~Bobbi, 66, mother of two

"It would be seeing my kids happy and accomplishing things, big and small, that make them proud of themselves from the time they are very little to now. And another would be spending good quality time with them as adults is amazing!"

~Rosanna, 61, mother of two

"I love getting to watch her grow and develop. The giggles, the adventures, simply exploring the world through the eyes of a child experiencing it for the first time."

~Elizabeth, 25, mother of one

"I love and appreciate all the phases of growing up. Each comes with its share of wonderment and struggles, but watching my kids learn and explore with their own eyes and figure out who they individually are was so interesting to me. Even now that they are adults, they continue to inspire me."

~Donna, 62, mother of two

"Getting to pray, care, support, love on, encourage, nurture, serve, lead, and help them."

~Amy, 53, mother of four

"My favorite thing about being a mom is all the different roles we get to play in their lives. We provide nourishment and shelter, comfort, then a nurse, teacher, chef, maid, counselor, disciplinarian, chauffeur, and finally a friend. I have enjoyed every single stage of their lives, and getting to be the different things they need at different times has been my most important job and greatest joy."

~Melissa, 37, mother of two

"I love seeing things through the eyes of my children. They add a spirit of wonder to even the simplest of tasks and experiences. It has been a joy to train and teach them. The fact that God entrusted the shaping and forming of these three little people to me has been the biggest honor of my life."

~Andrea, 53, mother of three

"When your children come back to you—full circle. When they finally understand the true meaning of love and how much you have loved and poured into them. When they finally understand the importance of family—loving and learning and being real and always being there for each other. I hope they finally get it—those very important lessons you knew they so badly needed for success in this life. It is answered prayer, a balm to your soul, and an absolute small miracle."

~Felicia, 58, mother of two

"Watching this tiny human learn about the world around him. Getting to experience little joys and discoveries through his eyes."

~Nadia, 24, mother of two

QUESTION 2–What is the hardest thing about being a mom?

"Letting go and letting them fly."

~Stephanie, 48, mother of two

"Wanting to do it perfectly (which I know is not possible)."

~Kirsten, 53, mother of one

"I never knew if I was doing it right when my kids were small."

~Kathy, 72, mother of two

"The heartache . . ."

~Tracy, 54, mother of three and two stepkids, five grandbabies!

"Not being in their daily lives anymore."

~Jenn, 53, mother of two

"Patience and trying to give them a better life than I had growing up."

~Jessica, 30, mother of three

"Losing control."

~Lisa, 47, mother of three

"When my children hurt, and it's not in my control to make it better."

Angel, 45, mother of three

"Letting them fail and problem-solve so they can grow and learn life lessons."

~Karen, 57, mother of three

"Having patience and staying calm and setting the right example for how they handle tough situations."

~Megan, 38, mother of two

"The weight of it all. Not knowing if what I'm doing is enough. Feeling like I don't measure up to other moms. Not knowing if they will choose to follow God when they are older."

~Kim, 42, mother of three

"The detachment from them as they truly expand their own wings."

~Amy, 52, mother of three

"The hardest thing about being a mom is giving my children grace and being able to accept that I am not always right. I also think it is hard to make time for myself and try to always do everything for everyone."

~Donna, 56, mother of three

"In the early years, it's the physical exhaustion and the anxiety of making decisions for their life. As they become adults, it's letting go and watching them make decisions that may cause heartbreak and pain."

~Beth, 54, mother of three

"So far, the lack of sleep."

~Emily, 28, mother of one

"Regrets. Wishing for do-overs, second and one-hundredth chances. Wishing I had done certain things and that I could undo others. Watching your children hurt and make hard choices and decisions. Not being able (or meant) to fix everything."

~Becky, 55, mother of two

"My mama heart wants to fix things when they go through challenging circumstances, but I've learned I can't, which has led me to greater trust and dependency on the Lord to resolve their situations."

~Shelly, 49, mother of two

"Seeing them make a mistake and letting it happen without interceding."

~Angela, 56, mother of three

QUESTION 3–Do you have a favorite Bible verse or quote, and why is it special or meaningful to you?

"Jeremiah 29:12: 'In those days when you pray, I will listen' (NLT). There have been many moments that I have prayed for my family and felt unheard, but in God's timing, He has always shown His faithfulness and plan."

~Kristen, 29, mother of one

"Romans 12:3–21. This is so important to me because it is instructions on how we should live our lives. I try to do the best I can as a mom of loving this way and have tried to teach my kids the same."

~Melissa, 37, mother of two

"Colossians 3:12–17 and Proverbs 31:10–31! The first scripture in Colossians speaks about the character of a believer, and the second one in Proverbs is the character of a godly woman. These are scriptures that I picture and use to steer my life."

~Gina, 57, mother of two

"Isaiah 64:8 is my favorite because the Lord has His hand on us all, shaping us and molding us transformationally to be more like Him."

~Jen, 51, mother of two

"'You knit me together in my mother's womb' is so special because I know God is the perfect parent."

~Kirsten, 53, mother of one

"Zephaniah 3:17: He delights over me . . . and he quiets me."

Alyssa, 38, mother of two

"Joshua 1:9. He is my constant companion in the highs and lows!!"

~Tracy, 54, mother of three and two stepkids

"Matthew 6:34. This verse has helped remind me that in the busiest seasons, it is easy to get stressed about what lies ahead, but it is important to surrender your worries and be present each day."

~Elizabeth, 25, mother of one

"Romans 12:9–10. The entire walk of being a Christian can be summed up in these two verses."

~Angel, 45, mother of three

"Habakkuk 2:2: Then the Lord answered me and said, 'Write the vision and make it plain on tablets that he may run who reads it.' I am also a writer, and God has been in each step of these children's books!"

~Karen, 57, mother of three

"1 Peter 4:8: 'Above all, love each other deeply, because love covers a multitude of sins' (NLT). We will make mistakes as moms, but we mother in love and with God's guidance."

~Beth, 54, mother of three

"One with very special meaning is a reminder from my mother: Matthew 17:20, 'Faith of a Mustard Seed.' She wore a mustard seed necklace around her neck, and I have one as well. It's a constant reminder of faith and my mother. She had thirteen children."

~Felicia, 58, mother of two

"Hebrews 11:1: 'Now faith is the assurance of things hoped for, the conviction of things not seen.' This verse has encouraged me in every season. And while it may have a different impact in different seasons, it always challenges me."

~Emily, 28, mother of one

"Psalm 23:2. I struggle to rest, and this verse is such a helpful and comforting reminder that God is the Creator of rest!"

~Nadia, 24, mother of two

"Proverbs 3:5–6. I sought to trust and depend upon the Lord for all wisdom and grace to parent and raise my children, trusting as we submit daily to Him, in all things, step by step, He will make straight our paths in following Him. We can't do it in our own strength and wisdom, nor do I want to try!"

~Shelly, 49, mother of two

QUESTION 4–What is the best advice or something you learned at this point in your mama journey you would like to share?

"Give yourself the same grace you give your children. Sometimes we don't get it right. Don't live in mom guilt."

~Kristen, 29, mother of two

"'Practice the pause . . . when in doubt, pause . . . when angry, pause . . . when tired, pause . . . when stressed, pause . . . and when you pause, PRAY' (Toby Mac)."

~Donna, 62, mother of two

"I know some people have different ministries that they are involved with, but being a mom and a wife should be your first ministry. Your ministry is to your family first!"

~Gina, 57, mother of two

"Pray for your kids and learn to communicate with them in a way that makes sense to both of you, where each person is truly seen and heard. Remember that Jesus is their Savior, not YOU!"

~Jen, 51, mother of two

"Give yourself grace. Just as your children are learning, so are you! You'll both falter sometimes and excel in others, but just do everything in love."

~Sue, 45, mother of three

"I have learned to treat my boys both separately as they are so very different and give them the space they need to make their own choices in life."

~Cathy, 58, mother of two

"All children learn and develop at different rates; they also have their own unique personalities. Comparison is never your friend."

~Elizabeth, 25, mother of one

"They are the Lord's, and He can take care of my kids better than I can—so surrender them daily and rest in Him."

~Lisa, 47, mother of three

"When they have something to say, stop what you are doing, look them in the eyes, and listen. Never be the first one to pull away from a hug, and if you feel it, say it. Tell them how much you love them every chance you get."

~Jennifer, 44, mother of one

"They have their own story. I can't teach them every lesson and thing perfectly to fit into eighteen years. They have so much to experience after they grow up as well. Give them a good foundation and know God will continue to guide and protect and teach."

~Stephanie, 48, mother of two

"It is true that time flies by so quickly, so I would say to young moms to enjoy every stage in your kid's life . . . don't rush through it. Be in the moment, put your phones down and give them your undivided attention. It will pay off big time!!"

~Rosanna, 61, mother of two

"Listen first. Children need to know how much they are loved so that they feel safe in this world and so that they can come to you with everything. Watch your words . . . they leave deep scars on the soul."

~Kathy, 72, mother of two

"We raise them to become independent."

~Jenn, 53, mother of two

"I don't want to be the reason my kids need counseling. You have to learn that there are different ways to parent."

~Jess, 30, mother of three

"Even though it's difficult to see your children make mistakes, we need to look at those mistakes as possibilities for them to grow in their relationship with Jesus."

~Bobbi, 66, mother of two

"To always remain grateful—grateful for the laundry and the messes and the making of the meals, and all the things, because it means I have two beautiful daughters I get to love on through the way I serve my family. We get to be moms, and it's one of the greatest gifts God has given us."

~Megan, 38, mother of two

"The biggest piece of advice I can give is to always cherish every moment you have. The newborn sleepless nights, the toddler tantrums, the awkward middle school years, scrambling to practices, and the teenager attitudes are all over in a blink. Enjoy every minute of it, talk with them the way you'd like to be talked to, take the time to do what they want to do even if you aren't interested, always make time for late-night talks, and remember the smallest of moments can be the biggest."

~Melissa, 37, mother of two

"Slow down. Have the devotional, play the game, watch the movie, listen to the story. Our children are such a gift and thrive when nurtured with love and attention. It will build a lifetime of the best relationship that will go from mom to friend."

~Kim, 42, mother of three

"Your children will make mistakes, and consequences are important to help them remember to correct their behavior and make better decisions next time, but there is also room for grace. The Father lavishes it upon us, and we can be generous with it too."

~Andrea, 53, mother of three

"Here is some advice I would like to share: It is so important to be slow to speak because you cannot take back the words that come out of your mouth. You also need to spend as much time with your children and grandchildren. Life is short, and you need to make the most of every moment. Don't get caught up with doing things that don't matter in this life. And lastly, always go on family vacations when you can because you will make the most magical memories you will cherish forever."

~Donna, 56, mother of three

"Cover your children in prayer before they rise and then pray with them as they leave for the day and at bedtime. Constant communication with God is a must in parenting and models the importance of prayer for your children."

~Beth, 54, mother of three

"There is no 'one-size-fits-all' way to love and parent our children. Each child and family is unique. Share your struggles. Ask questions and ask for help. Find/create a support system. Friends and mentors are important. Be willing to pivot and change course. Go to God. You do not only have eighteen years to speak into your children. It's different once they are older, but it still matters. Their growing up is bittersweet but beautiful. Be present. Be interruptible. These last two are my newest goals and desires."

~Becky, 57, mother of two

"Prayer is essential! I pray, pray, pray for our kids, their hearts and my heart. Guide them in the ways of the Lord and depend upon His grace for all things. Hold on to God's promises. Stay in the present. And pray, pray, pray!"

~Shelly, 49, mother of two

"Sometimes I see young parents so distracted by devices. I always shrugged when I was younger, and an older mother would tell me to enjoy my time but now I see it so much clearer. Don't let the distractions of this world cause you to miss the little things."

~Angela, 56, mother of three

QUESTION 5—Anything else on your heart that you'd like to share?

"Now that my kids are all adults, I find a different kind of joy being with them than I did when they were younger. Yes, time flies. But that doesn't mean you always have to mourn them growing up. There are rich opportunities for connection at all ages!"

~Sue, 53, mother of three

"Praying that these written words would awaken hearts to the Holy Spirit and a God who loves us totally and completely." (Amen! Thank you, Jen!)

~Jen, 51, mother of two

"I feel so blessed to have two wonderful, caring sons. I have realized that they both have very strong opinions, and I need to accept that they may not always agree with me. It's funny now I seem to get great advice from them both. They are definitely very independent thinkers and glad to know I can ask them for their feedback or opinions when I need them."

~Cathy, 58, mother of two

"My mom would always say to me when I left the house, 'Remember who you are.' I say that to my kids every time I hang up with them or they leave my home. As a Mom, I have to remind myself of this!"

~Sue, 53, mother of three

"I feel like since I have been a mama, I understand Father God's love for me so much more. There is nothing that they could do to make me love them more. There is also nothing they can do to make me stop loving them. There are so many beautiful parallels of the heart of God for us and a parent to a child."

~Alyssa, 38, mother of two

"I am so thankful God chose me to be my son's mom. I thank him for picking and blessing me with this honor. Don't forget to thank Him for hand-picking you to be your kid's mother. He deserves all the glory and praise!"

~Jennifer, 44, mother of one

"We need to let our kids be who they are—with loving guidance and lots of prayer. It takes time and error for them to figure out who they are. But when you have a relationship of love and respect, their mistakes may be less and their relationship with God and others will be ones of love and respect. The Lord created us all as unique individuals with unique personalities. We never want to try to change those core traits He created in our children."

~Bobbi, 66, mother of two

"We went to church as a family our entire life. I wish I would have spent even more time guiding my children in the Word. Nothing will ever be as important as living and following the Lord."

~Kathy, 72, mother of two

"Throughout the journey, He gives us many opportunities to trust Him . . . mothering is a high calling, one that requires us to lay down our lives and release our expectations to The One who loves our children beyond comprehension!"

~Tracy, 54, mother of three plus two stepkids and five grandbabies!

"They grow up so fast. They love you so much. They didn't ask to be here, so give them every reason to love being here. Be their safe place."

~Jess, 30, mother of three

"For me, becoming a mom for the first time didn't come easy. Many years of trying and disappointments when the fertility treatments didn't work time and time again. The miraculous day when I did finally give birth and held my son for the first time was the day that rocked my world. Now, my world is rocked again by the arrival of my first grandbaby girl. Seeing the light of my son and his wife in her sweet eyes inspires such a joy that only a grandma can know."

~Donna, 62, mother of two

"Relationship authenticity is paramount with children. They sniff out our stuff anyway . . . be open about mutual struggles, so they know you're a safe person to talk to and grow with."

~Angel, 45, mother of three

"Staying in community with other believing mamas is key. When lies come in, you have your sisters to remind you who you are, whose you are, and turn you back to the truth as you teach, correct, and guide your children."

~Karen, 57, mother of three

"Pray more than you say. Kids spell love t-i-m-e! Be present and love the season you're in (it doesn't last)."

~Amy, 53, mother of four

"As the kids have evolved into adulthood, I am reminded often that they are on their own journey. It's not mine." :)

~Amy, 52, mother of three

"Ask for help and take every moment to slow down and take in the joys of your child(ren)."

~Emily, 28, mother of one

"Unfollow all the mom advice accounts on Instagram. Get advice from people in your direct community, not from a place where all information is out there!"

~Nadia, 24, mother of two

***

I am believing many of these responses resonated with you in some way. We are all on a journey when we become mothers. Sometimes, that journey is riddled with difficulties and trials, but as we press into a compassionate and loving God, He will guide and direct us through these tough times. He will also redirect us when needed, as well as nudge us when we might be losing our cool too much as a mama. He is always there, providing redemption, reminders, and resolutions to whatever we are facing.

But most of all, He is there to help you rediscover YOU through all the seasons, and He helps you navigate those seasons so you are better prepared for the next assignment He has for you. Because if you are still here, He still has something for you to do. If you are still here, He still has opportunities for you to glorify Him. If you are still here, He still has lives he wants to intersect with yours. If you are still here, Mama, He's not done with you yet! So buckle up, give God the wheel, and enjoy the ride because He can be trusted with your life.

***

Seasons

By Renee Chenevey

S—Stillness in the Waiting
E—Eager to Change
A—Affirming God's Sovereignty
S—Solace in the Unknown
O—Open to new beginnings
N—Necessary introspection
S—Seizing the Lesson

(Written October 11, 2018)

About the Author

Renee Chenevey has spent a life loving the Lord after encountering Jesus at a Young Life camp in 1985. Her journey then led her into teaching and coaching for five wonderful years. While teaching she led a Fellowship of Christian Athletes group with students and was involved in Youth for Christ after school hours.

Growing up in the beautiful suburb of Hudson, Ohio, Renee excelled in all sports. So, naturally she found herself coaching basketball and track with her first teaching job in Canfield, Ohio. Coaching gave Renee a greater connection to her students as well as to her love of teaching.

She has always loved to learn and write. As a child she participated in the Young Author's program and had her first book made and then signed by illustrator and children's author, Steven Kellogg. This planted a seed for the hope to be an author herself someday.

Her educational background began with her undergrad at Grove City College, PA, and then she gained her master's degrees: one from Kingdom College of Natural Health (nutrition) and the other from Liberty University (education and English).

Renee lives in Medina, Ohio, with her husband, Jeff, of twenty-eight years and her two dogs. They are both enjoying a partial empty nest and embracing their new role as grandparents.

About the Illustrator

Hayden Chenevey is presently a graphic design major at Kent State University in Kent, Ohio. Hayden is highly talented in seeing and designing what works best, whether it's in social media production, photography, videography, Adobe Illustrator, or painting on a canvas.

His gift for design and creativity began in middle school, excelling in the required art class every year. By the time he got to high school, it was evident that God was leading him to use his gift in his future profession.

Hayden's other passion is going "into all the world to preach the gospel" on missions' trips. He hopes someday to intersect his knowledge and giftings from his college degree with supporting missions for all and contributing to necessary needs on the mission field.

Hayden also enjoys working out, playing sports, hanging out with good friends, worshiping, and spending time with his family and his labradoodle Duke.